Published in the United States by 2.13.61 Publications, Inc.

ISBN: 1-880985-59-4

Fifth Printing

Design: ENDLESS ∞

2.13.61
P.O. BOX 1910 · LOS ANGELES · CALIFORNIA · 90078 · USA

www.two1361.com

Thanks: Selby, Bajema, Shields, Vega, Carol, Dave, Heidi, Mitch Bury of Adams Mass.

JOE COLE 4.10.61 — 12.19.91

Maybe all presidents should be semi-literate, overweight and out of shape then they could always be remembered as "A true man of the people." If I was a woman these days, I'd be killing motherfuckers. My handgun would never cool and my hands would be covered in testicular blood. I would have a horrible reputation with a lot of men because I would be calling them on their weak bullshit left and right. Back when I was alive, I would always hear about how some woman was a bitch and then when I met her, I found her to be strong and not taking shit from the corny men around her. If you grabbed my ass when I walked past your desk, I'd make your brains come out of your nose. I hate seeing good guys having taking the rap for these weaklings. I hate the idea that any woman would fear me because she ran into the wrong guy a couple of times a day for a few years and thinks they must all be that way. What else is she to think? It is a failure. I know many men and women who had been married and had then gotten divorced. The levels of acrimony and ugliness at some of these proceedings alienated me from the idea of marriage. What a bad business deal. You get sued and all of a sudden you're paying money to someone you hate, who hates you right back. Maybe that's why men go to strip bars. Maybe women are safer when they are on display. Maybe that's why people like to watch pornography films. You don't get any on you, you don't get sued, you don't have to talk. Maybe most women should be either prostitutes, whores, strippers or publicists and most men should be criminals in cages, lawyers trying to get them out, pro golfers or politicians. Wouldn't that make for less paper work once the software was formatted? Everyone else could be employed to clean up after them. Maybe that's not such a hot idea, everywhere would be like Los Angeles. It was all a mystery while I was amongst you. I tried to love and failed. I tried to hate and got bored. Now I just drift through scenes and watch what you say and do. I write it down at night through a microscope. I turn specs of dust into planets, moments into eternities. I know that many married men have affairs. I know that from time to time women hate men's guts. I know the same goes for men. I know you think about sex all the time. I know you have killed people in your mind. I know that you say a lot of things to yourself that you would never say out loud. I know you say a lot of things you don't mean for fear of what the other chicken shit lying motherfuckers will say about you. I know you say one thing and do another. I know some of you hide behind the flimsy shield of political correctness. I know you, though. You want to fuck, own, and kill as much as anyone else. And all that, is what we have in common. One tragic laugh riot. No such thing as heroes, just crazy motherfuckers with good press relations. There was no "golden era" of anything, no such thing as the "good old days" because even then there was racism, rape and corruption everywhere. Maybe it's time to rebel! Rebellion? You mean that neurotic posturing you do before apathy sets in and *The Simpsons* come on? Virtue is a marathon. You're tired. I'm dead.

Walking point for no one. When I walk the streets, I avoid eye contact with people. I look at the street. I look at storefronts. I look away from their faces. When they see me, they call out my name and embarrass me. They are loud and stupid. I pretend I'm someone else. A guy named Ed. It works and I can feel myself relax a little and I can look up and out. I'm Ed. I stop acting like myself and start acting like this other guy. I am divorced from myself. I cannot be myself amongst them. I must be someone else. I walk and slowly forget myself. A block or so later I hear one of them yell my name like he's made a discovery and has to bring me up on charges of being myself. "Hey look it's _______! I can see you! I know you can hear me! Hey look, he's not turning around! Have a nice night!" I keep walking. I go into a store and buy a book. The lesbian is rude and goes out of her way to show me that she doesn't like me. I'm Ed. She has a problem with Ed. What did Ed do to this woman? Why do some people allow their sexual orientation to define them? At an intersection I turn the whole thing around in my mind. I don't care. I'm not Ed. I'm me, and I don't care what the fuck these people say or do. I'm so far from them. I wonder if the words that could come out of my mouth could leave lesions on their skin. I don't want to love anyone. I used to, but I don't anymore. For years I wanted to meet a woman who didn't make me want to be alone. I don't look anymore. I walk the streets, and I feel pretty good inside my distinct isolation. They know who I am. I only know myself. I hear them talk as I pass them. I listen to their words and try to imagine myself saying the same thing. I cannot. I have never felt farther away from humans than now. Every word that escapes my mouth is a solipsism. Every move I make is solipsistic. Solipsist. Look it up, insect.

I'm a veteran from another world and you'll never understand. The medals I was awarded are made from body parts of those who fell next to me. I threw them away as soon as they were given to me. Your words are useless to me, useless against me. Because the truth is that nothing matters. Nothing at all. From my window I watch a man sit in his backyard. He's there every day. He's barely visible because there's so much foliage surrounding the small cement clearing in which he sits. I don't know anyone who's ever spoken to him. Sometimes he reads, but most of the time he sits and looks at the ground for hours. It seems that either he knows he's being watched or he's used to being watched. He always holds the book he's reading in such a way that I can never tell what the title is. I never see anyone in the yard with him. He's always alone. I don't know when he leaves his house to get food. The shades are always drawn. No deliveries are made.

You'll never have problems sleeping again. I don't hate any of 'em. They're going to do whatever they get in their minds to do. I don't care anymore. You can call me and tell me you're not going to make it, that all the things you wanted to do will never actualize. That your dreams and ambitions fell flat and you got sold out by the fakes who you thought were so sharp. When you tell me you can't move because they drained all your blood and you're living in a commercial and you need their drugs to live through the day, that you need their lies to make you feel like you're alive—I won't tell you that you're fucked up. I'll just wish you luck. What is there to say? You're going to do what you're going to do. You know that laws have no meaning. They never stopped anyone from doing anything. Nothing can stop you from ending up the way you're going to end up. You look at all those people you said you would never end up like, and now you know them on a first name basis. They're not such bad people if you give them half a chance. In fact, you all have a lot in common. They make you feel good. They're not trail guides to the new nowhere, they're your friends. I don't hate you. I don't know you. As you're falling off you'll see that my arms were too short to catch you anyway. You'll end up right where you're supposed to be. Don't be surprised when you get there. Everything you did was a step in that direction. There's no such thing as bad luck.

I've brought some more people over to fuck you. You used to be so slick. You got tired. They wore you down and they changed your mind. Standing in the parking lot of the supermarket feeling lucky that you got there before they put the locks on the liquor section. Your shine is gone and the nights show on your face like never before. A whole new you. A new dead mask for you to wear the rest of your life. The soles of your shoes are thinner than ever and the insulation on your soul is so thin that you finally discovered you had one and its back is broken. Hit the bottle harder and ignore the laughter of the losers that are a few years behind you as they move the shit they used to say behind your back and re-locate it right to your face. They laugh at your tough guy act and fill you with so much fear you'll think you invented it. Tell yourself you're not weaker than you used to be—you're just smarter than you ever were. Stagger home and ignore it all. Now you're living. The Marlboro man is a grinning skull mask of hatred.

Misanthropy never felt this good. I like to listen to the music of the dead. I don't care much about the rest. In this room late at night, dead far away music matches how I feel in this world. I don't care about what any of these breathers are talking about. All they're into is cheap little get-offs. They can't hold me. When I play Thin Lizzy, Charlie Patton, Eric Dolphy, I separate myself from the rest of them. I am alone and that's fine. No one to talk to means no one to have to listen to either. Nothing to complain about. If you stay away from people as much as possible, then you'll be alright. Dead writers take me to a different world. That's how I deal with this one. I see no merit in facing off with cheap tin men and their straight-to-video homicidal trips. Like you really want to matter to some idiot. He can call me whatever he wants. I don't care what he thinks about me. He's not even alive in my world. That's it, they're dead in my world. All extras in a corny movie. People will just break your heart and kill you. The dead can't hurt you. You don't have to waste time talking all the common bullshit that passes for conversation with them. It took me many years of getting knocked around to see that you're better off on your own. Never getting married, never having children. Imagine someone calling me father. Never happen.

You see these losers and their miserable lot as they walk around shopping malls pushing baby carriages all over the place.

You see a man and woman together. Both out of shape and disgusting. They no longer care about themselves. Inside they know it's over. It's not me. It's what I see. Can't handle me? Can't handle the truth? Does it matter? Not to me.

The one who's going to survive the contemporary city environment is the one who can live alone. No spouse, no payments to the ex. I watched my parents' marriages. By the time I was in 3rd grade, I knew what the deal was. I knew I was never going to get married. It weakens men. They immediately lose it. Even if they have a close relationship with a woman, they slip. Often it's barely detectable, but they slip. Those who slip can die all too easily these days. I've said it before and I'll say it again, some things are really over.

I'm going home now and bleed from my head for awhile. Earth is huge and you'll never hear all the stories. Too much. Forget the Guinness Book of Records. He's eighteen and writes telling me how he killed a man over drugs when he was sixteen and just got out of prison. He's been using drugs since he was eleven. Pain and rage are all he sees. How does a country produce a man like this? What an industry. What a business. It makes me lonely and hollow. I don't want to know anyone. I don't want to hear any more stories. It's not helping. I don't need luck or friendship. I feel trapped with all these people. Wrong planet. Wrong time. I'm all I've got. I'm beyond it now. There's nothing you can tell me. Killing at sixteen. New American. New breed. New animal. Evolution pulling out the stops. This is what it comes to. All these dirty little creatures. I wonder what comes next after all the sadness has been drained from the seas and all the bullet casings have rusted. You can't kill a scream. It only dies when it's good and ready. And even then, it's always self-murderation.

Don't start with the "I love you" routine. My soul just got back from the cleaners. I've been working at it, and I've been getting stronger. For me it's always been about being able to take the pain. The more I can take, the safer I feel. I lift weights to the point of exhaustion and extreme pain. I sit alone for hours getting used to nothing. I have nothing to prove to them. I represent nothing. I am the ambassador of nothing. Finally. I get off on surviving. It's the purest level of life I have been able to find. When I say surviving, I don't mean just barely getting through the day. I mean surviving hard. I mean outliving them. As the civilization grows weaker I grow stronger. I am the inverse universe. I am a different species because I am evolving as they go DEVO. I am evolving in my sleep. I rely on biomekaniks and learned behavior. I am a biomekanikal man. Fuck instinct. Only criminals, war vets and wolves know instinct.

So I sit alone. When the urge to call someone arises I wait for it to pass. Take the pain. Get stronger. Get off on strength. Get high on strength. Fuck these half-people, half-insect fakes. Tiny words. Shit talking. No action. Fuck you.

Falling backwards from the force of the blast. One guy sends a hollow-tipped bullet that he was going to put through his head. At the last minute he took it out of the gun and sent it to me, first class mail. This bullet sits next to the bullet I found on the sidewalk in front of my old place in Venice. In a coffee mug to my left sits leaves covered with blood from a friend who was shot four times by a cop he was attacking. Next to that is a container with brain tissue from a woman who shot herself in the head. Upstairs is a plastic container with dirt that holds the blood of a friend who was shot twice. I have bars on my windows. Motion detectors in the hallways. It's past midnight and I want to walk to the store. It's 1990-something, so I don't think I'll go out there and take the chance. I got a letter from a guy in prison a few days ago. He told me he forgot what it's like in "the free world." I didn't know there was one. I wrote him back. I might as well have written a letter to Mars.

Civilization finally hog-tied by morality, imprisoned by its bogus pursuit of virtue. The criminal with the ability to kill without regret as the acknowledged highest form. Evolution out of breath and unable to keep up. Natural selection on overdrive. Survival indeed.

Give them bombs, they'll drop them. They'll create enemies to insure peace. Give them a grain of sand and some scientist will find a way to make it cause cancer. Progress means you'll live longer if we don't kill you better first. Freedom means you can be a killer, too.

What would you be like if you weren't distracted by the threat of violence? What would sex be like without the fact of rape or viruses that kill?

You can make all the technological advancements you want. Ten thousand new shades of red, Dinosaurs on movie screens, a new implant. You can do all that and say we're living in the age of miracles. You can hand out awards and talk about the future until you fall over. But you can't bring my friend back to life. All the plastic surgery in the world couldn't take the bullet hole out of his face.

The only thing we have in common is fear. Your gods are weak. Your music is weak. Your culture is weak. You can't make any of it look good to me. I don't associate with cowards. Don't call me your brother until you drop the gun and break it into pieces.

The gunman came from behind. The gunman was more than a man. He was a gunman. Equipped with brutal technology. He made a slight adjustment to local history when he shot the father of two in the back of the head for no apparent reason. He's a gunman. That's the reason. It was his genetic imperative to kill. Logic: I have to shoot you. I'm a gunman. I don't hate you. I don't know you. I will kill you and I will not go to hell. I will not "pay for my crime." There is no price to pay. I acknowledge nothing I do as criminal. Whatever happens is the truth. I judge not myself, nor who I have killed. Human life, like any life, has no value except moral value. Nothing could be more worthless than moral value. I am beyond morality. Many of you attempt to emulate my actions. You silently applaud me with your fear and fascination at what I do so effortlessly.

I don't want to talk to you and I don't want to mess up your carpet. They want to see what you've got. You sat in your room thinking about this moment and how hard you would kick their asses and now the time has come and it's nothing like you thought it was going to be. You forget all the lines you had saved up, all the things you were going to say to try and be so cool. All the time you spent prepping yourself isn't doing a bit of good. You thought you were going to be so smooth and now you can't even get your mouth open. I blew it by underestimating them. I sat in my room and inflated my ego instead of preparing my spirit to be strong enough to be able to handle anything. I went for ego instead of strength, clarity and spontaneity. They played me like a deck of cards, and when they were tired of the game, they shuffled me and put me back in the box. I shouldn't have bothered. I already played my own damn self before I even left the room. Nothing will ever turn out like you think it's going to. The truly great ones are the ones who can deal with it and come out smelling something close to a bloody rose mixed with sweat.

I let my shift manager feel me up. He gave all my friends free pizza. Sometimes you need to hide yourself from them on order to get an idea of who you are. There is such a thing as being too popular, too good, too right on time. When they come to depend on you like that they also come to lean on you like that. Soon they'll come to crush you like that. The more you take the weight, the more you lose yourself in their problems and insatiability. Sometimes a friend isn't a friend. Sometimes a friend is a bad thing waiting to happen. You need to get some time to yourself. When you feel the need to bolt—bolt. Most of this shit you work out on your own anyway. You know what I'm talking about.

Said the Abyss to Hamlet. Don't look too deeply into me. All I am is nothing and nothingness. I am but endless darkness and relentless silence. I am unmoving yet no dust settles herein. There are no answers here, warrior. Break your catatonic stare. Act now. Leave me forever and with the rest of your days, strike hard and decisively. Why let your fury lay deep inside you, sullenly boiling your blood into silent steam and grinding your bones to dust? Is it not better to thrust it out with great velocity from every pore, with your every action? Let your actions speak your legend. The physical is the manifestation of the spirit. Let your spirit be teeming with fury. Let your strength be unusual and controlled. The average is the borderline that keeps mere men in their place. Those who step over the line are heroes by the very act. Go.

I know I made a great mistake. I feel like a soldier who went to the jungle thinking that he was on the right side, fighting the good fight. Now I see that I gave a lot of years and a lot of blood to weak fools and leeches. They have since come back to try to break me. Little do they know how strong the years have made me.

Robert "Rob" Fulton. Ceaselessly destroys his life. Self-medicating, he lives to erase himself. Almost gone in what will prove to be his last summer. Portrait of an almost dead man in a dark room. In darkness I am safe. In darkness. I feel good and cold, alone and dead. I can see my fingers in the light that comes though the window. Overhead, I hear police choppers. The traffic roars and howls.

I'm past it all, way past it. Seen enough to know that I can't win. I can't even play with them. They'll just kill me to prove they were right about something. It means everything to them to be right all the time. For myself, I don't care. I don't have a personal anything. It's just another thing for them to come and take from you and shove down your throat. The less you have the less they have to hurt you with, that's the way I see it. I don't like it when they hurt me. It's all I can do not to mutilate them.

Is it a shame that I can't accept love? Am I too burned out to move towards what will keep me alive or too smart to get pulled into someone else's world? I only feel safe thinking of death. It's all I think about these days. I look at people. They don't know what I know. I talk to them they have nothing to tell me that matters. What is important to them means nothing to me. I am from another world. In their world I am extinct. I was murdered years ago. I look right through their brains, out the back of their heads and fix on the beyond. Once you're down with death, you have something that keeps you distant from others because you know what's around the corner. When you see people go by you can tell who knows and who doesn't. You don't want to know the ones who do because they are involved with the same nightmare you are. You don't want to know the ones that don't either because they are prey waiting to get taken out. You're alone all the way.

The times I have tried to get close to someone resulted in me feeling threatened and weak. When you allow yourself to trust someone, you never really do all the way, so why lie? The fact that I sometimes get lonely infuriates me. I hate loneliness because I see it as a weakness in my armor. When I'm strong, they will not be able to hurt me. When I let my guard down, they will try to hurt me, kill me. When someone tries to be nice to me, it makes me mad, mad to the point to where I say things to get them to never come near me again. When a woman shows me kindness the only thing I can think of doing is humiliating her before she does it to me. I am mean to her for all the ones that have caused me pain and confused me in the past. It is the coward in me standing up demanding to be recognized.

I immerse myself in pain so I will always be ready to deal with the pain that will ultimately brought upon me. I know they will, especially women. My mother hurt me and the rest of them will too. I don't think they mean to, it's just the way they are. They're all like my mother to me.

I hear all those blues songs about "where has she gone?" and all I can say is, who gives a fuck where she went, where she is or what she's doing. She can go any place she wants. I don't care. I don't care if I never see her again. I never even knew she left. Kill the dead man. Go ahead, try. Try to kill me. Put the dead man in pain, go ahead, you can't put me in more pain than I'm in already. Only in pain do I feel normal. It's when the pain relents that I become alarmed. That's then they might try to test me, and I always have to be ready to be tested. You never know what the little shit heads will throw your way next.

Outside of the room you take your chances with whatever they want to do to you. You can be victimized by a weak piece of shit too easily. You have to be ready for whatever they want to bring your way. You have no control. Laws protect them from getting what they need. They can talk to you or try to touch you and you have to be able to deal with it. Some guy was talking shit to me last night, and I wanted to punch him in the face as hard as I could. I didn't do anything. You can't do anything to them. They just use it against you. They can take their weakness and shove it into your guts and make you look like a fool. And all of a sudden you're doing time in their jails and doing everything that they tell you to. They win. When you play the game, they always win. I always feel like I'm getting fucked whenever I leave this room. When I go out there with them I get raped and there's nothing I can do about it. I am held captive by my own strength. Held down by my own rage.

All the people that made a difference in my life have either died or left me. So the rest of them I don't care about. I don't play that game anymore. I did before and I see where it got me. The truth is the truth, they're all the same. People are created equal. They act the same, feel the same and respond the same way to the same things over and over. How can I care about one of them and not care about all of them? How can I not care about any of them and yet care about one or two?

On this endless night, I am thinking about this woman. She made the mistake of trying to get close to me. I let her get there because I figured she must be doing some kind of research project like that lady from the University who did the report on me. When I found out that she actually felt something for me, I was immediately filled with contempt for her. I told her not to depend on me for anything, not for any kind of commitment, comfort, anything. I told her that I am just a stupid animal and will only cause disappointment. Finally I could no longer speak. I felt so dead inside that all I could do was hang up and make the room even darker. I came to the conclusion that I don't care about friendship.

I don't care about most of the things that I used to. I don't even care much about living. I'm just here until I die. I'll just sit in this dark room and wait for death to take me. He's busy right now but knows right where I am.

I've been running for years but I'm tired now. Tired of all the bullshit. Mine and everyone else's. I've been spending a lot of time thinking about how I ended up like I did. How much of me is me and how much of me is an imitation of my father and mother? I see the characteristics. When I used to talk to women I could feel my father rising inside me. He was a loser too. He tried to do the right thing but he was a loser. Losers know things that winners don't know, will never know.

All this running place to place, just to end up and then taking off for the next place. I see what a load of lies it can be. You can move fast and keep the lies at bay for awhile but they catch up with you and then you're done.

I feel good in the dark. I like the lights off so I can see if anyone's coming. I don't like people being able to see me going past a window in this place. I don't want to give them an edge. I have worked a long time not to give any of them the slightest advantage.

I close my eyes in the darkness. In the silence, I can imagine some kind of relief. Usually some scene in the desert. Sitting in the middle of a black nowhere trying to think about nothing. Trying to get a few breaths in before the horror comes back and my eyes grow wide and vacant, filled with the Abyss. I would hear a shift in the sand, look around and a woman would be there. Someone to tell a secret to. Someone who would be a friend to me. I would talk; she would talk. All of a sudden, the mask falls off and it's my mother sitting in front of me laughing, her teeth falling out of mouth and the smell of men coming out of her skin. I open my eyes again and I'm on the floor in the dark. I feel safe in the dark because if someone breaks in here I won't be such an easy target. In darkness I can forget myself. It's the only way I stand a chance. You look at some and you know they're marked.

I spend a lot time living in shadows. I am hoping that they will rub off on me and I'll become a shadow myself. It would be great if parts of me would go away and never return. I am one that goes through the motions. I have not felt whole for ages.

I got my heart broken. My spirit got shattered and mutilated. I will not be coming back from this. I don't want to. I am so far up the river now that there is no coming back. It is possible to know too much. Experience leaves scars. It has proven to be my undoing. You can still function as a living ruin. It's easy to hide it. But those who know can spot it on you in a second. They're broken as well so they just look on and move past you, another shuffling ghost. The last thing they want to do is know what you went though because it only reminds them of the living hell of their own lives. They are happy to leave you alone.

Another night is upon me. It's the time I like the most. It's the only time I can deal with the city. In the light I feel like I might get mistaken for one of them and I will get taken into their hell. I have one of my own. If I didn't get out of their world I wouldn't be alive enough to write this. Don't call me "Rob" in the obituary.

Man chained to a television set in a hotel room in Moscow. I watched a man on television talk about OJ Simpson. He was superimposed over a back drop of nighttime Los Angeles. I could see tracer bullets coming from the LAPD choppers as they randomly fired into the ghettos. Small explosions jumped up from the ground where vehicles were hit. The man spoke about OJ's plan to release a fragrance and a clothes line after his acquittal. The screen cut to the place where Simpson's ex-wife was found murdered. The amount of blood surprised me, the color too. I'm only used to seeing blood in movies. I think I prefer movie blood over real blood. Movie blood is just plain better looking. The news program got off the OJ thing and went on to show some footage of life in Haiti. I couldn't understand how those children could smile so much. Next they did a report on sensuality. They asked Cindy Crawford a list of questions about what she thought was "sensual." At one point her lips became so large they obscured most of her face. Black liquid started to come out of her ears. A high pitched scream came out of her mouth and she started to shake uncontrollably. Maintenance men came and whisked her away. A large man put his hand over the camera lens and they cut to a test pattern. Then a commercial came on for a machine that strips paint off surfaces. A buxom woman holding the item smiled at me. She had a tight yellow shirt on that said "Easy Stripper." After that, the news came back on and talked about a luxury train you can take through northwestern Mexico that offered deluxe accommodations and exotic cuisine that included the flesh of children and road kill.

The pungent smell of an assassination attempt. Shoot. Score. What were you thinking? Did you think that they were all like you? You were wrong about that one. Concentrate on the agent's shoes as he stands over you. Wait for the ambulance that will take you to the ER of the local hospital. They've seen lots of gunshot wounds like yours. You're nothing out of the ordinary. Do you see it now? Do you see now that your self-righteousness was nothing more than breeding and years of privilege? "You know, we are one nation under a god." Yes, you were right. An angry, crack slinging god who decorates with bullets and spent condoms. A blind god whose eyes are just like yours. The bullet in your hip is freedom's back hand. You should have brought your bulletproof life with you for this one. Not everyone is equipped with factory standard morality. You're not picking up any votes today. Hey, I know. To stave off the shock, think of a cool mantra to chant before the press gets here. How about, "More cops, bigger armies, one god, no problems." You're drifting... Wake up and smell the blood. The press crews are here. They beat the ambulance. God rewards in the strangest ways.

Get ready for the machine that eats humans. Americans are at war. Right now, somewhere. They always gotta be stomping some motherfucker into the dirt. Do you ever wonder about the long term effect of that? You have to get ready for the maniacs. Someone hasn't gotten what they deserve and they will be coming to you with generations of confusion, animal need and pure rage. It will be an epic-while-you-wait. You might just want to start torturing yourself early on so when the real thing comes your way, it won't hurt as much. If you haven't been raped yet, you can go to a rape center where men will rape and assault you at gun point. I can get you thumbscrews cheap. You can do it at home by yourself. Survival is all about preparation. I paid a man to strap me to a chair and make me watch surveillance camera footage of clerks getting shot in convenience store hold ups. It taught me a lot. By the fifth hour I was hallucinating about a better place. Coming down was hard but you know that you have to some time. I feel sorry for the ones who aren't going to make it. Not everyone will and that makes me sad. Start mutilating yourself now. "Make it hurt now so it won't hurt later." Learn to fear willfully. It's easier on the ego. You can convince yourself that it was your idea.

A noose of blood to end a life of hope. When you hear screams coming from down the hall, don't be afraid. It's only me trying to get the ghosts out of my guts by beating my flesh with my fists. When you're about to go to sleep and you hear strange growling sounds coming through the wall, don't think you're in danger. It's just me trying to talk my blood cells into shooting themselves in self-defense. I'm packed with broken glass and memories and it all hurts. I'm breeding scars in here. I'll sell you one cheap. Wrap it around yourself like a shield. You can wear my pain and it will seal out the pain others try to inflict. It will help keep the world from turning your mind into a slaughterhouse. If you find blood on the bathroom mirror, don't worry. It's only mine and I can take a lot of pain. I'm good that way. I'm bad the rest of the ways. I carve my face off every night to make masks. You can have one. You can wear it on the street and no one will know you're you. Then you can be yourself instead of the other person you pretend to be when other people are around. The mask gives you freedom. Use my pain. Benefit from my cowardice. If you pay my rent for another month, I'll hack off one of my hands and you can use it to kill someone. Leave it at the crime scene and they'll never catch you. Use me. I have no use for myself.

One of Fear's delicate tendrils. Weak now because you own. You possess. You have something they can take. Remember how it was when you had nothing? You looked at the ones who had what you wanted and felt strong in your need. Brave in your limited surroundings, righteous in your desire for something different and contemptuous of those who had exactly what you wanted. You hated them because they looked weak and slightly scared. You circled the water hole and thought about closing in. Now you have what they want and feel weak in your capacity to keep it. You feel desperate to make them see that they take it away. It's yours. You never had to justify yourself and your possessions before. "I earned this. I worked hard for what I've got. I paid my dues. I deserve this. It is mine." Sounds like tin words spat into the wind. The animals circle and wait. Shake your fists at the hyenas. Chase them away from your water hole. Justify. See them all differently. Now you see that they all want something. They want exactly what you got. Human gets some juice. Human becomes prey. Human gets scared. You figure out that you have to be hard to keep what's yours. You have to be cruel. You have to kill them off just for looking. Leave the bodies by the water hole so the rest will see. Hang spent bullet casings from fishing line outside all the windows of your house. Put up signs "Please break in. I would love the opportunity to kill you legally. I want to hang your fucking skull on my front door." Let the fear turn into desperate anger. Start seeing the differences in people. They all start looking suspicious. They. All. Want. The need never stops. Out there, someone is always needing. Always hungry. Always looking at you. Checking your eyes for fear. Zeroing in on the vein in your neck as they circle the water hole and close in. Funny that after all the years of struggle, your triumph results in you living in one small room of your big house, tired and sick with fear, cut off and alone. Only the strong survive and you're not anymore. Check the windows and doors and wonder how much more time you've got before they come.

Check the gate! I read about it in Rolling Stone Cold Bore. I'm supposed to feel something for a groupie who made her living sucking porno stunt cock and spent her time chasing rockstars? She couldn't handle the money or the drugs so she took her head off in her garage. Took her nine hours to die. Tough. Read the tragic tale of a young girl who grew up and took her self hatred to the small screen. What you people do to yourselves and each other... you're so weak. Some of you should win awards. I think it's great that you watch films of people fucking each other. I think it's great that you can't get it happening for real so you have to watch. I think it's great when the talent shoots themselves in the head. That's my kind of evolution. There's no such thing as tragedy, just dumb motherfuckers being themselves and suffering those slings and arrows. All you do is watch avidly. Nine hours to die? She could have taken a couple more loads in the face before then. They may have even rolled film instead of that beta crap.

Dear Savannah. I don't know how to start this letter. This is the third time I have written this letter and this time I'm going to send it! I bet you get a lot of letters from men telling you that they think you're beautiful how they want to fuck you. I don't know if you'll even get this letter. If someone else is reading this, fuck off!! And don't send me a fan club thing either. I am a real person. Well, if you actually do read this, I just want you to know that you have had a large impact on my life and I just want to thank you for all the good times you have given me through your work. I have a bad job and I live alone. I don't talk to my parents. I hate my boss. I was in love with a woman and I told her I wanted to get married. She said that she loved me and agreed. I found out later that she was fucking my friend Tony from work! I told the both of them to fuck off!! I don't know what happened to them.

This is where you come in Savannah. I got turned onto your films by Tony, of all people. Your films give me hope that I might meet someone as beautiful as you someday.

I know you're busy and you probably get letters from people like me all the time but if you have a few minutes to take out of your busy schedule, maybe you could write me a letter. I'll put down my phone number at the end of the letter, call collect anytime! It would be an honor to speak to the great Savannah!

You are the most beautiful woman I have ever seen. I really hope you get this letter.

Did he say the song was called "Enter Sandwich Man?" *Is there any life after self-contempt? Is there anything as satisfying as the feeling of rage and fury coursing through my veins?* He walked across the kitchen and looked out the window at another apartment building. *How can I get through the next three to four decades of my life with this constant thought nagging me?* He stared at the floor and listened to himself breathe. *People spend too much time trying to make themselves happy. They never know what it's like to feel the sheer, silent weight of existence. They're too busy running from something that they haven't even dealt with. How can they be the masters of their own lives without this knowledge?* He stood and silently questioned himself for another fifteen minutes. He looked at the clock and figured it was a good time to go to the store and get the food gathering ritual out of the way before all the freaks filled the aisles. He couldn't stand to look at people in the market. The way they needed an entire aisle to walk their cart. The horrible food they bought. He imagined people putting this wretched food down their throats for years and it made him sick. They didn't get it. They didn't see it. They didn't even know they were alive. They were too busy rushing home to get wasted on bad food and television. His mind shifts to a vision Roseanne Arnold. She comes into the living room, takes off her clothes, gets down on all fours and eats food that's strewn all over the floor. People from the market come in with their shopping carts of bad food, nude up, throw their food on the floor and join her. It's nothing but fat white flesh and the sound of foil and cellophane ripping. All that soft bread. He got his coat and headed for the store. As he walked down the street he noticed there was no traffic. He looked up the street and saw a roadblock with some policemen standing by it. As he stood staring, a man passed him and said, "Some kind of march. Fags, I think." The market was full of the freaks he was trying to avoid. It was almost as if he was on the set of a bad movie and had the entire cast to himself. They were just as he knew they would be. Babies crying. Fat women in bright colored stretch pants. He wondered how women who looked like that could ever get a man to get naked with them. "Desperate," he said out loud. Soon the food gathering ritual was over and he was in line to cash out. He always picked the line with the funny guy at the register. The guy was a riot. He cracked jokes non-stop and rarely did any of the customers get them. The checkout guy liked him because he could hear him laughing a few customers back. "Ah yes, ice cream today; you're healing nicely from the last time I saw you. Here's what's left, don't spend it all in one stall." All the cashier ever got was a blank stare and an outstretched hand awaiting the change. Whenever they saw each other they gave each other a conspiratorial nod. "Hello. Bullets half off today." He got his change and left. He was walking up the steep incline towards the street when a carload of young men pulled up along side him. "Excuse me mister do you know what time it is?" He looked at his watch and then looked up at the young man who was smiling and looking slightly downward. He followed the young man's gaze and saw a small caliber handgun pointed at his midsection. He didn't say a word. He forgot to breathe and when he did, it came out spasmodically and he simultaneously released a small jet of urine that immediately showed through his trousers. "Look man, he pissed in his pants!" the guy said and started laughing. "Do you think you're gonna die, bitch?" the guy asked. The man said in a hoarse whisper, "Please sir, don't shoot me." The young man looked at his friends and repeated the sentence in a high pitched voice and all of them started laughing. The boy's face went from a mocking leer to cold fury and he shot the man in the upper part of his right leg. The car peeled out with a lurch and nearly took out a car coming into the lot. The man was surprised that he was still standing. He stared down at the rapidly expanding red circle on his pant leg. He walked back to the store with an almost trance like gait. When he was a few steps away, he realized he was still carrying his groceries. The security guard was staring at him with a blank expression. "I've been shot," the man said and looked down at his leg. The guard looked at the wound and said, "Hold up a minute," and walked into the store. He had to get out of the way of a woman coming out of the store with two children and a full cart. He found himself saying, "Excuse me." He stood with his groceries wondering why the bullet wound didn't hurt more.

Is that anonymity rock? Well turn it up, man! It took me an hour to get the nerve to leave the apartment. I usually only go out at night to avoid people. In fact, I have changed almost everything I do to avoid people. I spent a short time looking in the mirror, making sure I didn't look too strange. I have a tendency not to look into a mirror for long periods of time and have learned that a little rehearsal is good before going out there. I practiced smiling in case someone recognized me and said something where I had to respond in a friendly manner. I rehearsed it like an actor gets ready to do a scene, because when I'm out there, it's all a scene. It's all acting. I said a few words out loud and stretched my mouth so I would be able to talk with ease if I had to. I go for long periods of time without talking and I have found that I lose the ability to speak with ease if I don't warm up a little. Finally, I had my act down and was ready. I had my route mapped out. I take the darkest streets for as long as I can until I have to walk on the main blvds. Minutes after leaving my place, I was on the big street. Whenever I see people coming towards me, I instinctively look down and away from them. Tonight was pretty good, not many people on the street. I got to the record store and went into the classical section to acclimate. Not many people are ever in there at one time so it's a good place to get ready to have to see and hear a bunch of people at once. I faked like I was reading the back covers of Beethoven CDs until I felt ready to go into the main part of the store. I steadied my breathing and went in. I thought I was going to be able to go in there and be alright. I was wrong. The place was packed with people and I immediately forgot every CD I was going to look for. Out of nowhere an employee called out my name and asked me if I needed help finding anything. I wanted to speak but all that came out of me was a grunt and a slight shake of the head while I stared at the floor. He went away. I felt like I was the only one who had a Halloween mask on. I walked idly down the aisles looking through sections that didn't interest me, pretending to look engaged while I was trying to remember what it was that I had come in for. I heard someone behind me say my name. My hands turned into scaly claws. I could feel an extra set of arms pushing against my sweatshirt. I turned slightly and nodded, and hoped he wouldn't see my hands. I managed to find the records I wanted and get to the cashier's desk. Two of them looked at me and smiled. Antennas popped out of my head. "Is that all for you tonight?" I managed to nod and smile; it seemed to work. I passed for normal for a second. It's like getting a phrase right in a different language; you study and it pays off. The man behind the counter started telling me what he thinks of the things I have done and there's a line of people behind me waiting to pay and leave and they can't because the young man is still talking to me. Every word feels like a hot nail driven into my skull. At this moment, I want to run out of the store and leave the CDs. I feel their eyes at the back of my head. I wonder if anyone is going to hit me. Finally he lets me go. It was like being let up for air after having your head held underwater. I walk outside and see a place where you can get coffee and sit outside and it looks like a really good idea. I am walking by thinking how great it would be to just walk in there and get a cup of coffee and sit outside and drink it. Just like a real person. I look at the inside of the place and then look at the seats and see that some people at a table are staring at me. One is pointing and another is laughing. It's time to go. I do my best to look like I wasn't interested in going in there in the first place and walk to the street. The hand that isn't holding the CDs turns into a hoof. A girl seated across from a guy sees it and coughs a mouthful of coffee into her napkin. I walk quickly to the street. I get a block away from the place and I hear a man call out my name. I turn around and he comes up and tells me that I kicked him in the head when he was nineteen. I struggle for something to say but the only word that comes out is, "Good." He says he has a son now and he is also a fan of mine. I recover in time to attempt to use humor. "Well, bring him over sometime and I'll kick him too." I laugh, he laughs. I do the smile that I practiced in the mirror and the wave that I saw in a movie and keep walking. That's a wrap. Good scene. I hit all the marks, my timing was excellent. He probably thinks I'm a pretty good guy after all. I make it back to the dark street without much incident. I walk along wondering how men meet women. When I go out there I see so many of them together. What do you say? Do you walk up to them and ask them if they want to go somewhere with you? Don't they yell rape and run away? Don't they just laugh in your face? Probably not. I come to the conclusion that if you hang around other people long enough you're bound to bump into another one who might be interested in spending some time with you. Seems pretty hard to believe, don't you think? I know that women would be able to read me like a book. They would ask me what I did that day and ten words in they would all of a sudden remember a place they just had to be right then. Doesn't really matter does it? Just do what you're going to do and get on with it. Less talk the better. I don't complain, I deal with it as best I can. Sometimes I do alright, sometimes not. I get back to my room several minutes later. The room has no windows but I can hear traffic, police helicopters and sometimes people. I listen to the CDs I just bought one after the other like I'm taking a required course. They sound ok, I guess. I don't know for sure because I have a high pitched ringing in my right ear that never ceases. It's the first thing I hear in the morning and it's the last thing I hear at night. Too many nights knocking my guts out for the approval of strangers. I am an idiot and totally responsible for the misery that descends upon me regularly like a squadron of hungry vultures.

Sitting like a glass of water in the middle of a dark room. I have learned the way of silence. It is sharp and beautiful like a katana blade. Never tarnished by time or conflict. I have been ushered into the dark world of silence with a hero's welcome. Four in the morning, awake. Not waiting for anything. Immersed in silence. Eyes steady. Sitting microscopically in the great expanse of silence. When I leave my room and go into their world, I am filled with silence. I stand in its shadow when I to talk to them. I hear their words through a filter that is silent and devoid of light. They ask me how I am and I always lie. No one really wants to know how you are unless your health status benefits them. They're just exercising a ritual that they're not even aware of. It's always alright to lie in this situation. I tell them I'm fine from ten thousand miles back in the fields of silence. What I really want to say is, "How am I? I am present. I am being. I am at all times." Their world confuses me and makes me feel strange. I love to look at their women. So beautiful and alien to me. I read about myself in their newspapers. I talk to their representatives and do my best imitation of a human. They say I'm pretty good. I imitate their gestures of gratitude and retreat to the desert of silence. It is there

I have learned that I am a fool. My desires are foolish. The things I want are better kept to myself. The hand of silence is steady. The hard blade of silence is clean like night. The code is absolute. Silence is eternal and patient. Silence never makes a fool of itself like I have so many times. I told the nonsound that stands before me that I only meant to do good deeds. The silence stood unmoved. It does not judge me but merely waits for me to see the mistakes I made. The message I get is that I don't have to right my wrongs—just don't commit more. If I am to give anything to their world, I should only give my silence.

I am holding your head like Hamlet holds Yorick, but I have you on your knees with a gun in your mouth. You have heard the saying that those who don't study history are doomed to repeat it? Yeah, well I was thinking that maybe we should tear up all the history books and a few drug crazed nights from now, we'll think that we made all of this up. If we have to keep repeating it we might as well take some credit. Fuck Plato and all those guys. Tear up the great works of art. Destroy all the ancient ruins—fucking ruin 'em! Dinosaur bones? We'll burn them for fun. Who cares about something that was living fifty million years ago? You don't know if you have five minutes left. Let it go. Stop trying to know every damn thing that ever happened! What's your problem? Stop being victimized by all this dead stuff. Let's take the world back! No more living in the past! Burn all the films. No more sports or television. No more recorded music. Fire all the executives. No more dyed hair. No more fake tits and nose jobs. If you think you're ugly, just deal with it. Roseanne Arnold, we're gonna pump all that fat back into you, graft pieces of your prodigious ass onto your face to make up for all the tucks and liposuction, and restore you to the pig you really are. No need to hide! You won't have anyone to impress. No ratings to worry about. All the televisions will be gone. No studio to go to, nobody to boss around and intimidate to make up for the insecurities in your life. Be what you are! Stupid white trailer trash! Don't be afraid! No more tabloid photographers, we'll break their cameras. Now you can be real, like the person you pretended to be on screen! No more politicians. All offices will be ransacked. Hey man, inhale! You have no one to account to now. World leaders? Fuck 'em! You'll never see them again. All the airplanes will be destroyed by rioting pilots. No more jobs, no more job discrimination. No more layoffs! Sexual harassment? Hey, if he grabs your ass, take him out in the parking lot and bash his fucking skull in! No more religion! Basically, men are afraid of women and can't handle the fact that they came out of the same thing they spend the rest of their lives trying to get back into. Pathetic or what?! We'll take it from there and make it up as we go along. All we'll have left is sex, food and killing. Let's stop making movies and start living in them damn it!

How to eat your own flesh and not freak out. Everything you do makes my body scream with loneliness. When I see you, the room swallows me. I find myself at the bottom of the pool. I can see leaves floating on the surface as I black out and regain consciousness again and again. If you touched me, I would grab the sharpest thing I could find and mutilate myself as quickly as I could to fill my body with pain so I could balance out the pain that your eventual absence will leave me with. A night with you is savage. Two lifetimes compacted into a few hours. It gives me brain damage. Doesn't last long though. Soon enough, I find that I am a stranger to you and homeless in my skin. My wall is marked with blood spray and holes that fit my fist.

Herb, I got it! Schindler's List 2: Triumph of the Will! Think of the crossover potential! You came into my room. Immediately you felt your muscle tissue slowly start to dissolve. It's the room eating you alive. You put your hand on my shoulder and screamed when you saw the smoke rising from our flesh welding. That is my desperation trying to make you stay. I know you'll never love me but maybe you'll stay for awhile. You try to speak but the only thing that comes out is the sound of the jungle being skinned alive. We attach by our teeth and try to destroy each other in an attempt to keep from destroying ourselves for a few hours. Thank you for touching me. Some of the only moments worth living were spent with you. Not you especially, the collective you. Different faces. Same pain. Dark, hungry rooms all over the world.

The "A" side of the single had a long title: "The Ears of My Relatives, Both Close and Distant, Carefully and Lovingly Strung on a Single Leather Thong (Swinging Gently in the Breeze.) The "B" side was a sloppy version of the Beach Boy's classic "I Know There's an Answer" from their groundbreaking *Pet Sounds* album. If the world gives you the blues, if you wake up in the middle of the night with waves of fear and senseless panic washing over you, I am your friend. If you're overcome by a desperation that makes your mouth open for a scream that never comes out but just freezes your face in mute despair, then you and I have something in common. If you can't understand them for the life of you, even though you've tried so hard, when that dislocation makes you feel like you're the only one of your species on the planet, I know I can confide in you. If this endless ghetto of lies and heart break, this life-long run of fences and flickering neon signs, night sweats and suicidal urges makes you feel like stopping, just stopping, like stopping breathing, wait. Wait. You don't have to tell me your name. You don't have to prove yourself to me. I accept you. If you're finding life to be the one thing that's trying to kill you, I want you to stay alive to rise with the sun and fight back.

I don't know why it's now that I think of you. Of course, I am with someone else. She is lying beside me, cold. She has been dead for a few hours. We broke into this place this morning and no one knows we're here so, when I leave tonight no one will find her for quite some time. I have pretty much forgotten about her even though her body is lying here. I did not kill her. She killed herself. I met her yesterday on the strip. She doesn't matter to me. You do. She's dead and gone and a stranger as well. You were never a stranger to me. I always felt I knew you. You didn't want me and I was mad for a long time but now I see that you could never be with someone like me. I know you don't hate me either. I have not seen you in years but I always think about you. I hope you're alive. I don't know anyone who knows you. I'm moving pretty fast these days but I think of you still. I had been visiting some friends in Portland. I was taking a much needed break from my overdriven work load in Los Angeles where I was employed as an editor at a variety magazine that I am too ashamed to mention here. The money was amazing but I couldn't look myself in the mirror sometimes. I was hoping it was going to be a temporary gig. I was lucky to have a job in that city at all. Getting back to Portland was the reality check I needed.

One of my friends invited me to a party. It was small, about twenty people. Much smaller than the see-and-be-seen scenarios I was still not getting used to down south in my adopted smog-ridden home. From the minute I walked into the room and saw her, I was in love. I had to endure the entire evening being the only person in the room who knew this. I tried to speak to her but she was not interested in talking to me. I quickly lost my courage and left her alone. She left in the middle of the party. I asked the host about her but he didn't know who she was and neither did anyone else. We all thought someone had brought her and it turned out that none of us had. That night, I thought about her as I tried to sleep and figured the best way to deal with it was to forget her and move on. As the day passed it was all I could do not to think of her all the time. Even months after my return to LA, I was still thinking of her and her disappearing act.

Imagine my surprise when I walked right by her on the sidewalk near my office. I thought I must have been mistaken but I wasn't. It was her. I asked her if she remembered meeting me in Portland at that party and she nodded yes. I asked her if she lived in LA. She just shrugged. I was too busy looking at her eyes and her mouth to ask her what she meant. You would figure someone would know where they lived, right? I asked her if she lived in town and she said, "I'm in the process of moving." I asked her if she would go out with me and she said yes. She said she would meet me at the restaurant we were standing in front of at seven and quickly walked away. I didn't get her name and now that I think about it, she didn't smile once.

The five hours until seven crawled. I couldn't believe I had seen her again. The chances of that happening were next to impossible. It made me think of all that stupid crap like destiny and karma.

At seven she was standing right where I had encountered her before. I asked her name and she said it was Louise. We went in and sat down. I tried to get her to talk to me but she only answered in short sentences. She worked in video sales but didn't tell me anything more than that. I asked her where she lived and she replied that she was thinking of moving to San Francisco or Los Angeles. I asked her if she lived in Portland and she said, "Portland, please." I found that odd. In fact, everything about her was odd. She never asked me anything, so I started talking about myself and you know how fast you bury yourself when you try to make yourself sound interesting, especially to someone who just stares at you. The whole thing was going nowhere. I wanted to tell her that I had been thinking about her nonstop since the night we met but couldn't find the words. She excused herself and went to the restroom. When she got back I would tell her everything I had been going through. I would force a reaction out of her with my truth and passion. It sounded lame but it was all I had. So I waited. After twenty minutes I asked the waiter if he had seen her. He said he had seen her—he had seen her walk out the door right after she got up from the table. I paid and left.

They say that true love only comes around once and you have to hold out and be strong until then. I have been waiting. I have been searching. I am a man under the moon, walking the streets of earth until dawn. There's got to be someone for me. It's not too much to ask. Just someone to be with. Someone to love. Someone to give everything to. Someone.

Ok, tell me that you don't want the story to end. Tell me that you really feel for me and want to know what I did next. Tell me there's a happy ending. Tell me that this meant something to you. Tell me that you're not laughing at me right now. Please don't be laughing.

The only safety is in the middle of total misunderstanding and deception. Right now I'm in a train station. I'm surrounded by a bunch of loud, beaten down travelers. The place I'm sitting in smells like a latrine. Every breath pollutes me, makes me sick, makes me hard. But it's all right. The noise and the hustle beats me down but it's not so bad when I compare it to a life of living off the actions of others. A vicarious existence that fills one with hate and envy. I think I'm better off out here. Out here, there's nothing but strangers. I'm one of them, moving namelessly through the night. Every time I think of home, my throat gets tight and I want to get on a train and move on with the strangers, leaving our names back there. I'm riding in a train. It's dark outside. The windows are black. Who knows where we might be? I start imagining if the windows were really black, and there was no one in this car but me, I could ride for years. I could ride through an endless night. No chance. Sun will be coming back in a few hours, bringing the colors and the pain. But now, swaying through the night, the dull roar of the engine cools my head. I can imagine I'm being shot down the barrel of a gun, a long black barrel, a bullet without a name. Swaying from side to side, without hope, without a prayer, without a doubt. A desperate traveling stranger. Endless black night train ride. My hand presses against a cold black window. Sad train, heavy ride train. I've got a thought like a frozen stone. I tell you, that's my heart right now. Beating frozen man, dead life rhythms. In-out all the time spinning sane-insane sane-insane revolving door madness inside my brain. No answers. To ask a dead end mind. Cold air black train ride tonight.

You don't see me. My mind projects erasing thoughts into your brain. All traces of my image disintegrate as soon as you come in contact with me. The more you look, the more you don't see. Sometimes the small animals I killed were so beautiful that I carried them around for a few days until they started to stink too much to hide from my mother. I had a dead bat for three days and it stunk up my whole room. My mother came in and asked if something died in there and I told her no, I killed it outside. I had a dead kitten that I killed with a rock. I kept it outside so my mother wouldn't give me grief about it. I would come home from school and play with it and watch it rot. I found a dead pigeon and hung it up from a light pole. It stayed up there so long that finally the weight of the body pulled away from the head. This all leads to you. You're beautiful like those animals were. You have pretty eyes, your hair smells nice. Mean things come out of your mouth but I'm used to it. The snakes and the turtles and the bat all tried to bite me before I killed them. I feel safer touching beautiful things after they are dead. When they are alive they don't let me get close. They either run away or tell me no. NO. DON'T TOUCH ME. NO. I DON'T WANT TO TALK TO YOU. NO. I DON'T WANT TO KNOW YOUR NAME. NO. GET AWAY FROM ME OR I'LL SCREAM. For a minute, I thought you were different than the other ones. I wanted to believe it so bad. You hurt me but I still think you're beautiful. You're like one of those beautiful animals and I want to cut your head off so I can look at you for a few nights before you start to rot. I could carry your head around in a bag and show it to people. I could ask people if they wanted to see something really beautiful but it's a secret. They would say ok because everyone says they can keep a secret even when they can't. That's when I could show them your fuckin' head. And when I'm tired of looking at you, I could take the bag and swing it at a wall as hard as I could a lot of times and then you wouldn't be beautiful anymore and it would feel good because it would be me who made you dead and ugly. Then I would feel safe and free.

Love is self deception. I am a living creature. Hate is only self love. I am a double feature. Sometimes the only thing that is amazing to me is my ability to disappoint myself. To think so much and try so hard and get almost all the way there and then feel myself falling backwards to where I was before. The lump rising in my throat as I realize that I am all the things I hate I must like it. That I really am set in my ways and going to be a loner all my life. That there will be no intervention by someone else. That all the love songs were written by people who never lived them. I like to listen to them because I can always turn them off. I like the idea of someone else's love safely sealed in a song or a book. I know that mine will always be rooted in hatred, contempt and fear. It's been years since I had a dream that didn't involve work or some level of panic. I see my ultimate failure mirrored back in the eyes of those I know. In their expectation of me. In their honest love for me. It makes me want to warn them to get away because I will disappoint. I will betray. I will turn vicious and not remember why or when. I will never be able to tear myself away from the dark, violent sickness of my life because it's the only thing I know. It is what defines me. I associate it with my parents and all the pain and horror of youth. I only feel safe in my solitary sickness where the only one getting hurt is me. I know that I will eventually hate them and do my best to make sure they feel the same way about me. They saw potential in me and they are going to make me deliver and I just can't face that. So sure am I of my ability to fail that when someone tells me I can do something else, I can't hear it. Tonight I am alone and thinking about your tears and pleading. When I said I never wanted to see you again, you clung to me and your crying made you convulse. I could feel your tears on my neck and your hot breath on my shirt. I knew that I would never be able to say aloud what I just wrote here. I knew it would've come out mean and wrong. I knew that nothing I said would ever get it right because who would believe it? If you felt the same way you would have seen me in yourself as soon as we met and you would have avoided me. That's why I cut you off before I started in with the sick undoing of your ego. The nonstop manipulation and dependence. It's what I know. It's what I like. I'm only going to tell you this once.

Keep walking, empty eyed man. The first feeling I ever had that I felt was my own was when I was young and riding my bike at night. The sound of the tires on the street and the wind rushing by my ears made me feel good. I felt strong. No one could tell me what to do. I noticed that all the kids around me were always with other kids. I never saw a person my age walking alone. I hated boys my age. They would tease me and beat me up. The humiliation was hard to take. I would eventually learn to engage them in episodes of violent fury that they always regretted. I learned there is a lot of strength in having nothing to lose. I saw early on that I was always going to be on the outside. I knew this by the time I was twelve.

I started to think of myself as a person from another planet. My hatred for people grew more intense as I grew older and understood more of the ways of the world. I was done with my parents by the time I was sixteen and only listened to them so I could remember what to say and what not to so I could get around them with more ease. I never did anything to make them proud or impressed with me. I never thought they were anything more than people I was staying with until I could get loose. I never learned about their lives and to this day I know nothing more about them than I did when I was a teenager. I do not know when either of them died.

As the years passed I grew farther and farther apart from my parents and the kids in school. The only thing that brought me back a little was the pursuit of women. I always felt that women belonged to them and that they could tell I had spent most of my time on my own and therefore was a loser. I had almost zero social skills besides those which I learned from watching television shows. I knew life wasn't like that but I tried to affect the cool of the people I would watch. It did nothing more than alienate people further from me.

As I got older and started living on my own, I remained a loner. The farther away I got, the more natural it felt. I can still hear the wind like I did on my bike over twenty years ago when I walk the streets alone. When I am near people, I can't hear the wind. Nights are wasted when spent around others.

The years passed and the jobs and addresses changed. I drifted all over America, never staying in any one place for more than a year. The scar tissue on my eyebrows and knuckles became deep lines on my face and hands.

I learned to forget. I learned to hear the sound of the wind rushing by my ears even while working in a mail room or some dank factory. I always lived alone. Friends came seldom and went quickly. After awhile, I stopped looking for company and just thought about it as I walked the streets at night.

I eat at this one place a few nights a week. Usually there's a man sitting in the corner table reading a book or a newspaper. One night he came over and sat down across from me.

He leaned over the table and looked directly into my eyes. I could see the pain in his face as he was trying to find the words. He looked away and sighed deeply. He spoke quickly and quietly. "I've seen you in here a lot. I'm checking out soon. The Agent Orange is pushing through my chest bad. I don't give a fuck. Marine?" I shook my head no. "Doesn't matter, fuck it. Here." He handed me a piece of paper and a war medal. I looked at the medal, it was a Purple Heart. He looked at it and smiled. He shook his head, said, "Fuck it," got up and exited the diner quickly without looking back. I read the piece of paper. Blue ball-point ink, barely readable.

"This may come as a relief to you... you will always be alone. Crowded rooms, busy streets, it doesn't matter. Your solitude will be with you always. You will wake up alone mornings of all four seasons and go to sleep the same way. The years will pass and you will witness your body slowly showing the ravages of time. Of course, there will be the intermittent crossing of paths with women. Be assured, all these liaisons will be short-lived. If you are not immediately distracted and alienated, you will find yourself filled with contempt, either real or imagined, soon enough. You have seen too much. You know the wrong things. Experience is a well-dressed curse. The higher power has a price. The price is the silence of truth. The ghosts never leave, the echoes never die down. They know you better than anyone ever will. Until you stop fighting the reality of your life, you will pass the nights looking for someone else to share your isolation with. You will never meet your equal because you have none. You will only be reminded of your discontent, hence your emptiness and contempt while in the intimate company of another. You are uniquely damaged. It's the scars that keep you from ever getting away from what you know, what you are. The sooner you learn to accept your fate the better. The time passes easier, you stop tormenting yourself. I know how it is sometimes, trust me. There's no one who understands except other people like us, ones who are damned and know it. In my company there is no solace because all we have in common is the abyss which fate has cast us to walk forever through. You always walk through it alone. This is life's sickness. This is the joke life plays on us. Look too deeply and regret forever. I know you know all this shit. I'm dragging this motherfucker all the way down the drain. Fuck it!" No signature.

I left the note and the medal on the table after I finished eating. Didn't mean a thing to me. Never saw the man again. I have learned to forget. I forget it as soon as I learn it, I never actually know too much at any one time. There's nothing or no one I want to know. I don't ponder the great mysteries of life. I don't think there are any and if there are, so what? I don't wonder when I'm going to die. I don't read books, watch television or go to movies. I just work, walk and sit. I don't hate people like I used to. I don't remember when I stopped. I don't remember when I stopped being proud of anything or feeling superior to others, either. I have never told anyone I loved them except for my parents and I only said it because they did and it seemed like good idea to repeat the phrase back to them and not encourage discussion. I didn't feel anything when I said it. Love never seemed like anything I ever needed. I just move on, live through it. Watch the seasons, walk the miles, survive the time.

Not disabled, unable. In my dream I die and come back as a brick. Yes a brick. The brick I come back as is lodged in a wall that was built in 1951. My exposed side faces the window of the woman I love who turned me away years before. Day after day I stare into her room, into her life. I watch her come and go. I see her with different men. I cannot call out, I cannot move. I am embedded in cement. I can do nothing but silently and motionlessly watch. I see her alone. Sometimes she cries and holds her face in her hands. I am forced to watch endlessly. Sometimes she stares out the window and looks right at me. It is excruciating to look directly into her eyes and know she does not see me; she only sees a wall. She leaves for weeks at a time and I wonder where she is. Who she's with. I wait. All the other bricks are just bricks. They do not speak They don't do anything at all. It is only my discontent that makes me believe that I am alive at all. I have no arms or legs. I feel neither hot nor cold. I do not sleep. I do not hunger or thirst. My face is a small rectangle of smooth red clay, anonymous. Sometimes I think that I am a man merely dreaming of being a brick but the days pass and I can see enough to know that I am indeed a brick in a large wall. One day she moves away. Days turn into months and soon the first year of her absence arrives. In this time, I have done nothing but make up every possibility of her return to my view a potential reality. Five years pass. My mind has begun to drift. I watch squirrels and birds. A few families move in and out. I see a few traffic accidents, a robbery. Leaves explode into colors and fall off the branches. But at night when everything is quiet, I think of her. She is somewhere. I am here. Always here. Not waiting, just here. Please do not let me live my life untouched and tormented. Please help me escape the tragedy of myself. I envision my face: contorted and agonized, wild eyed, my mouth frozen in mid-scream. Never able to say the truth. Forever trapped. Suspended inside solid black eternity. Embedded, silent, identical to the hundreds of others, stacked symmetrically around me.

Drums made of human skin stretched over ribs beaten with severed arms. Playing all night, paying homage to love's annihilating, all consuming hunger. The dancers scream as the flesh melts from their bones. They rush forward, begging for extinction. I can feel the blood leaving my body. There is a pool rapidly forming around my midsection as I lie here on the sidewalk. I hear traffic sounds and I can see people peering down at me. People are talking about me but no one is talking to me. I am cold and alone. A moment ago I was walking. I heard gunshots and then something pushed me to the ground. Am I dying? Yes, I am dying. I can feel life leaving me. It's strange that amidst all the noise and confusion around me, I am clear headed and my thoughts are calm and rational. All I can think of is you. All the things that I never told you, how much you meant to me. I don't know why it is now that these things come rushing to me so clearly. It is sad that you will never know these thoughts of mine. The things I am feeling while I inhale the smell of car exhaust and blood. It just occurred to me that it is my blood I am smelling. You will surely find out of my death but not of these thoughts. I must tell you that I was always afraid of the fury with which I loved you. It overwhelmed me. I thought it beyond comprehension, therefore my silence. I felt overshadowed by the power of it, I was afraid of it and afraid of you. So strong and pure was this passion that it came out as pure venom. I know that you will always think I hated you. If only you knew how wrong you were. I remember when just the sight of you would send me into a fit of rage so blind and molten, I would claw at my flesh until I drew blood, hit myself in the face and cry. I remember the last time I saw you. You were so kind, and I was so hard and sullen. It was all I could do to contain myself. A rose trapped inside a fist. If I had not walked away quickly after my short reply, I would have been at your feet, begging to be at your side forever. It is the only place I ever wanted to be. To me you are more than a woman. You are a creature of beauty, a creation of a higher order. I will die knowing that no one will ever love you as I have loved you all these years. I will now attempt to say your name with my last breath.

A pyramid materializes at the intersection of 75th & Broadway. Traffic comes to an immediate standstill. People stand drop-jawed as the pyramid levitates and slowly begins to spin. The air becomes filled with a hum that increases in volume until people cover their ears and fall to the ground screaming. The sky becomes dark with swiftly advancing clouds of locusts. Behold Ra. I am lost without you. I have been staggering through life for so many years. I no longer know how to communicate. I don't trust myself around people. Am I paranoid? Have I been away too long? At this point I don't see how I ever... No, it doesn't matter, no meaning to be found in any of it. What I feel, what I know, what I have seen. It will stay with me and disappear into muted animal horror spasms before it goes to the safety of total extinction. To speak in confidence is so desperate, a mortal waste. Years ago I cared. Now I don't. I know I am lost but I don't want to be found.

Years of freedom only to wake up in your treacherous embrace. Free no more. To be loved. . . To be scalded and covered in cauterized flesh. From mother onwards. The end in sight always. Taste the fruit and wake up in a bed of snakes. Check the freedom in doorways and public parks. Living on the ground. Urinating on the sidewalks. Sleeping in the fetal position while civilization proceeds to demolish itself at breakneck speed. To be accepted by the murderous... No, not me. Not my life. I will not be bound by liars and death dealers. I will not be held to the ground by their tiny truths and muttered threats. I do not hold my life dear to me. I have never had an experience that made me love it. I have never thought myself lucky to be alive. I have never thought of survival. I must have lived all these years on instinct, denial and Darwinian knee jerks. I used to think that your eyes were jewels. I used to think your touch would heal me. I forget when I stopped thinking these things. I don't know why I remembered them at this moment. Perhaps it is the cold air. Perhaps it is the slate grey sky overhead. I saw you in a dream last night. You came at me with your mouth open in a scream that made no sound. I could not see your eyes. You always brought me pain. Stupidly I held on, even though I was shattered years ago. Increments of time that I smashed out of existence so completely I could be standing in front of you right now and you would not recognize me. Unwittingly, I healed myself.

I am the flying saucer man from another world trapped on yours until they come to rescue me. One day the saucer will land. Jimi Hendrix and John Coltrane will open the hatch and tell me to get in before someone tries to blow up the ship. I'll just ask what took them so long. Within seconds we'll be out of here. Quietly, I sit in the hotel room. The door has three locks on it. No one knows I am here but the lady at the front desk and she doesn't care. Traffic passes by the window. No one yells my name out. People pass my door in the hallway but no one knocks. **IT** The city glitters and blinks outside my window. It's times like these when life is almost bearable. No phone calls, no one's company to endure. I can think my own thoughts. Dodge their arrows and stones for awhile. People make me sad and lonely for solitude. **WASN'T** I feel better when I'm walking alone. I like eating alone. Movies are better alone. Alone is safer because you attract less attention and when you're alone, you're harder to figure out. You only have to look out for yourself and not worry if the person you're with can handle themselves in a bad situation. **SUICIDE.** I'd rather be outnumbered and alone than have a weak person with me. Music sounds better when you listen to it alone. It's great to look at paintings but only when you don't have to listen to them telling you their impressions of the work. People ruin almost everything. Being around people makes me think I have nothing and that I'm a creep. On my own, I don't feel half bad. **YOU'RE** I got tired of being a vulnerable idiot, telling someone what was on my mind. I got tired of humiliating myself over and over. Only a fool trusts a human. All you can do is predict what they will do next and prepare yourself for what might happen. Look at all the divorces happening. You would think that people would figure out beforehand that it doesn't work and just give it the slip. **GOING** I hear about people getting their bank accounts cleaned out because of a divorce. It's hard to believe that these people wanted to spend the rest of their lives with each other. Imagine the feeling of failure when it doesn't work. People spend years after divorces in deep depression. They have to go into therapy. They are mad all the time. Can't feel sorry for them—they bring it on themselves. **DOWN**. Waco, Jonestown, they always bring it on themselves. Then they'll tell you that if you don't get out there and at least try, you really haven't lived. Haven't really lived in hell you mean. Right now, in some city, somewhere there's a light on in a window. The curtains are partially drawn and you can't see in from the street. There's music playing and the door is locked. That's me.

I look at pictures of you because I am afraid that you would notice me staring in real life. I looked at your picture today for countless minutes. It is closer than I'll ever get to you for real. I felt like I was looking at a captured animal at a safe distance. If you knew I was doing this, you would feel sickened and frightened. That's why you'll never know. Years will go by and you'll never know. I will never say the things that I want to say to you. I know the damage it would do. I love you more than I hate my loneliness and pain. Somewhere someone is thinking of you. Someone is calling you an angel. This person is using celestial colors to paint your image. Someone is making you into a vision so beautiful that it can only live in the mind. Someone is thinking of the way your breath escapes your lips when you are touched. How your eyes close and your jaw tightens with concentration as you give pleasure a home. These thoughts are saving a life somewhere right now. In some airless apartment on a dark, urine stained, whore lined street, someone is calling out to you silently and you are answering without even being there. So crystalline. So pure. Such life saving power when you smile. You will never know how you have cauterized my wounds. So sad that we will never touch. How it hurts me to know that I will never be able to give you everything I have.

The sky didn't crack. No fire fell. The sidewalks obeyed me. The night did not move. I remained. Winds of February come early this year. Make it so cold they all scream and run away. Make it so cold they won't come out of their little holes for a few days. Let just the strong ones walk the streets. Winds of February, come forward and roar them into extinction. Kill summer madness with final death gusts of cold. Make the streets desolate. Make the nights clear. Make the nights the nightest nights ever. Make the star light cut through punishing frozen air. Make it so only the strong can see the beauty. Let the rest stay indoors huddled around fires cursing the weather. I will laugh and walk through the beautiful ghost town without having to listen to them pollute the remaining time I have left. Freeze my eyes. Freeze my heart. Turn my feelings into hibernating giants. Never to wake.

I want to be the king of the empty mind. I want to sit in front of you and be able to listen endlessly and not feel. I want to be boredom's master. I just want to walk with extinction for awhile, maybe for a lifetime. The anti-mind will be mine. I will nourish it with toxins and the light of black and white television. I am charged with electricity to make my heart run at a slightly higher rate. This ups my metabolism as well. This is good. I have to make new blood all the time. I have a lot of people who get their blood from me. The only hard part is the generator I have to lug around with me. It's an old one, weighs twenty-five pounds and gets pretty hot. I carry it on my back. People say I look like a hunch-back. At night, I run out of language pills and can no longer speak until I get another handful from the machine in the morning. **EINSTEIN**. I walk the streets carrying the generator, which makes a loud whirring sound, that has caused a large part of the hearing on my right side to go. People call out my name and all I can do is wave, point at my mouth and show them the "Out of Order" sign I wear around my neck. They understand and let me go on. The tubes that come out of my neck hurt sometimes. In the morning, they will attach themselves to the tubes and get blood. I don't mind, I guess. **MANDELA**. They seem to need it. I guess being healthy is a curse. I guess that being helpful makes you a sucker who gets leeched. I guess that being good at anything these days makes you a mark for people to eventually come to hate and plot to destroy, or in my case, slowly drain. It's alright though, I have them beat for now. With the generator and my fierce will to live, I can withstand them and their constant need for my blood. I don't think about people like I used to. **GHANDI**. I used to like them because I felt like I was one of them, but now I only feel like I serve them because I have more than the average person does. I have what is called, "Servant Syndrome" which is when the servant feels that he or she is superior to the one being served. I have always felt this way if you want to know the truth. When people come to me for a liter of blood, I can see the self-loathing in their eyes. They know their weakness and they know that I see it plain as day. Why else would they ever come to me? **OPRAH**. It's not as if they like me. They just get what they need and leave. One day I will run out and they will leave me for a healthier specimen. You have never given me anything. All you ever did was take and watch yourself in the mirror the whole time. I never was given a chance to give. The only thing I have ever done is get taken from. Every day, I endure the drainers.

We were marched into the walk-in freezer and told to face the rear wall. I remember seeing your breath coming out in short gasps. It reminded me of walking home from school on a winter's day. You looked at me and I remember the look of fear in your eyes. You were shot before me. I always thought you were brave and the luckiest of all of us. You didn't have to watch the rest of us executed. The pleas and the screams were unbearable. How I miss you. Autumn is here and the early darkness is depressing I know. Autumn is here and you feel absolutely no interest in going on. Ending your life seems like the best way to deal with the boredom and savagery that this urban failure brings upon you. It's this season that can save you if you let it. Hail the oncoming winter weather. Soon it will be silent and cold. The nights will be safe and frozen. Germ free. Humans are toxic but easier to take in this weather. Their smell is down somewhat. Don't end your life in a dimly lit room. Don't let the dead end of your job destroy you. The cold air is good for you. Walking alone is the one of best breaks you ever get. No one to have to put up with. No one to disturb your thoughts. No one to have to come home to. If you need company, you can always play an Art Tatum record. Fall is coming and the idiots are back in the suburbs they crawled out of on their insect legs. The wood burning fires are filling up the night air, making it worth sticking around for. In defense of the fall weather! Tip: <u>Don't blow your brains out</u>. Sleep is better in cold weather. Autumn is the time when a good book is a better friend than your fellow panicked urban compressionist. Falling leaves and grey sky is the time of the greats; Poe and Dostoyevsky come alive on cold nights. Raskolnikov's madness will speak clearly to you. Knut Hamsun's character, Nagel, was always a cold weather man. Company is nice, but only if they keep their mouths shut and leave when you want them to. And since they never do, let's leave them out of this. The summer leaves me feeling old and wrong. It's only in the Autumn where I can take breaths that make me want to take more breaths. This is important. I know that most of the things I am trying to do will end in total failure and disappointment. I know I will have a later life that will be bitter and full of regret. I know that many of the people I worked hard to please will let me down, as I will eventually let them down. I see that no matter what I do, I will always be solitary and somewhat tragic. But I will always enjoy the grey solemn solitude of this season that grows darker and colder, day by day. The season that seduces and prepares me for the greatest season of them all. Winter. The season of heroes and gods.

The beautiful scarred ones went all over the land, setting buildings on fire and breaking clocks. All structures became an endangered species. Time was destroyed. Real life rose to power. They became true gods, immediately. There is no time to spare. There is no time to waste. There is no time at all. There's no need to speak. We will communicate by touch and instinctual expression. We don't need words. We're well past all that now. It is our destiny to be born beautiful into an ugly age. We breathe life in the face of Death's high command. It is your animal grace that keeps me alive. It is your feral eyes and taut skin that brings my veins to the surface. You are beautiful like demolition. Just the thought of you draws my knuckles white. I don't need a god. I have you and your beautiful mouth, your hands holding onto me, the nails leaving unfelt wounds, your hot breath on my neck. The taste of your saliva. The darkness is ours. The nights belong to us. Everything we do is secret. Nothing we do will ever be understood; we will be feared and kept well away from. It will be the stuff of legend, endless discussion and limitless inspiration for the brave of heart. It's you and me in this room, on this floor. Beyond life, beyond morality. We are gleaming animals painted in moonlit sweat glow. Our eyes turn to jewels and everything we do is an example of spontaneous perfection. I have been waiting all my life to be with you. My heart slams against my ribs when I think of the slaughtered nights I spent all over the world waiting to feel your touch. The time I annihilated while I waited like a man doing a life sentence. Now you're here and everything we touch explodes, bursts into bloom or burns to ash. History atomizes and negates itself with our every shared breath. I need you like life needs life. I want you bad like a natural disaster. You are all I see. You are the only one I want to know.

Loneliness is the exposed throat begging for the blade. Hardened alienation is the cold, thick skinned hand closed around a coffee cup in some lit box on the desolate planet. Once you're one with it, then you know nothing else. The old life fades away like a forgotten sunset. The new knowledge creeps in unnoticed. You are there. Mysterious night blooming flowers explode though the cracked and hardened face of the concrete below my hotel window. I am triple-locked in my maddened, lonely room. Stifled by my own presence. The anti-sunlight blooming flowers will cushion my fall when I jump out the window to meet the city tonight. It is the only way to represent my desperate will to live in these pointless times. I live to extract love and beauty from these sagging ruins. But only at night. I live only to see that which goes unseen by the rest. Their color television radar paranoia registers obscure most of these things. Night lets me breathe and exist how I want to. I take off the mask and live for real. The deep indigo colored air waits for me outside the window. I jump and the lush vegetation anticipates my descent and enfolds me in a lush, verdant embrace upon impact. I am silent and alone. The way I was born to be. Years ago, I thought I was born to be struck by lightning. Now I realize that I was born to be unshattered and undistracted by constant travel across unending tortured roads. Born to become friends with exhaustion and the smell of diesel. Somewhere along the way I lost hold of their language and customs. I listen to them as I pass them in the night and I can't understand what they're saying, or why they do what they do. Was I ever like them? What did I want out of life? What did I think it held for me? Was there ever a point where I knew it would end up like this? Did I ever see this coming? One thing is for sure. I am here and I am this way. I have ended up. Mystery has turned into exploring the night desert of eventuality. Every night I walk the streets. Every night I wish I was walking on the moon.

Your eyes change minute to minute. Your beauty spreads itself out like a painted fan. The more I look, the more I see. Your beauty perches like a butterfly on a flower. But the flower is melting ice poison and the wings are razors. I reach to touch and the blood falls in silent room drops. My feelings for you shame me into silence. The truth of this and your name will never be revealed. It is you who has made me realize the failure of my life. The thought of you fills me with longing and at the same time, a burning humiliation that produces scar tissue and dead brain cells. Your existence mocks me and I am unable to confront this. You have no idea of any of this. None of this is your fault. It is completely with me. It is you who makes me see what I really am. I am weak and out of touch with myself. I am disturbed and unwilling to summon the courage to overcome the demons that perversely allowed me a glimpse of true love, only to rip it from my grasp. I walk the streets knowing that you exist right now. How many hours I have thought of you. Conversations I have made up while moving silently through cities all over the world. How well traveled my thoughts of you are. I am sure I am not the only one. You are the untold story. You are the impassioned truth wanting to scream its existence, to be forever trapped by a strong hand clapped firmly over the mouth of my soul.

We waited willingly to drink the toxic water. We stood all day while the jets passed overhead and shelled the city randomly. With locusts crawling all over us, we waited patiently. Even when we saw the others who were ahead of us going into convulsions and vomiting blood after they drank, we waited breathlessly. We were so thirsty and besides that, we wanted to get close enough to see you smile. I don't think any one of us minded dying that day. I want you to know that if I had another life to live, I would have done it all over again the exact same way. I watch your mouth move. I listen to your voice. I do everything you tell me to. Minutes later, I find myself sitting on a metal chair with my hands cuffed behind my back. I tell you this is the second time that I have been handcuffed in my life. You say nothing but your expression makes me understand that you don't care. I don't mind being in this position because I trust you, and even as uncomfortable as this is, I don't mind because it's time spent with you and any time spent with you is special to me. You ask me why I love you and I tell you that no one talks to me like you do. Some of the best times I have ever known are when you call me and we talk late at night, they are . You smile and ask me if I want to kiss you. I tell you that I want to kiss you every day for the rest of my life. You lean in close to me and lock your eyes onto mine. You open your mouth slightly and move in closer. In the instance before your lips touch mine, I see the glint of the cobra's head inside your mouth. You pull me to you, clamp your mouth onto mine and the cobra goes down my throat, followed closely by a few more and then several scorpions. You pull back. I can feel the creatures in my guts, biting and stinging. I ask why you have done this to me. You say, "You're just mad because I don't want to fuck you." I tell you that I don't care about that and why did you hurt me when I have never done anything to you. You pull out a knife and start stabbing yourself. I tell you to stop. You tell me to beg you. I beg you. Tears stream down my face. The pain of the snakes and scorpions are forgotten, all I can think of is your safety. You say, "I'm showing you how weak and stupid you are." I black out. When I awaken, I am on the floor of a hotel in the middle of nowhere. The rug is warm and I am glad to be alone. I look up to see the door and to my great joy it is triple locked. It's the first thing I do when I come in, never knowing how the curse will manifest itself. Whatever happens, no one can be here unless it's a dream of you or a cobra you might send to keep me company. Alone is perfect because it's all I can handle. I was never able to deal with company who stays too long, unless it's you with your flesh melting words. Almost everything and everyone outlasts their welcome. Human nature is anti-human. I dream of anonymous room numbered nights on flat ground near major highways. I always stay below the windows and I never answer the phone. I know it will never be you.

You forgave me in a dream the other night. The more you told me it was alright, the worse I felt. I know that you were only doing it because you knew I couldn't possibly hurt you more than I already had. I could see what forgiving me was doing to you. I know that you think I'm too stupid to figure it all out. When you forgave me, you knew that it was finally over. The pain would leave me, I would forget you and you would never see me again except in a dream. It is sad that the things that we saw in each other are no longer there. It is a shame that we tore each other apart looking for things that we needed desperately but could never find. It is tragic that we only wanted to give to each other but only stole from ourselves and blamed each other for the emptiness in our lives. I see you differently now. I no longer fear you. It took years to see you for what you are. I no longer associate you with screaming and dry heaves. **HOW MANY NOSE JOBS NOW?** You know what? I see now that you gave me the courage to addict myself to the sickness your presence in my life offered. The puking and blackouts were just some of the slight side effects from the heights of crippling pain you inspired me to climb. Years later, when scars were all I had to show for the time I spent with you, I would dig at them to make blood come out. **FOUR?** It made me feel closer to you. I would be alone in a room, several thousand miles away from you, screaming and bleeding and wanting to die but now I see I was just trying to get back to you. **CHIN REDUCTION, LIPOSUCTION, BOOB JOB**. Yes, I am ashamed, but it's the truth, so there's nothing I can do. When I saw you recently and you put your arms out to embrace me, I cannot describe the joy I felt when my flesh started to tear away. So many years alone gouging myself and the whole time you were waiting to have me back. Your voice of one thousand black night ravens. Your soul erasing eyes. I can't believe I survived without you and with all the pain you caused me to inflict on myself. **FACE IT BABE, YA FUCKED UP**. Can you believe that for a time I hated you? That I wanted to see you dead? And when I didn't want to see you dead, I wanted to die myself. I used to spend days at a time thinking how nice it would be to not exist. I wanted to die because I blamed myself for all the endless hatred you poured on me. Now I see that we need each other. All those years I spent away from you. I hate to think of how you got by without me to burn and scar. I hope you don't think that I abandoned you. I was selfish. **AND SOON THE WORLD WILL LAUGH AT THE TRAVESTY YOU HAVE MADE OF YOUR LIFE**. Now I only want to be near you and give you everything. It's ok to come out bright eyes. Sit here. Now like before, talk to me real nice and gently drain the blood from my veins. Help me destroy what is left of my life with your neurotic, insane screeching. Infect my thoughts so that everyone I meet will seem strange and threatening, causing me to alienate them. Your lips are thinner now that you're older but they still pull back from your teeth when you're about to strike, just like they used to in my dreams. Spend a little more time with me so that my last years will be bitter and wretched. Pass every confusing, enigmatic facial expression of yours on to me so I will see it on the faces of others and always blame myself. Tell me that it's going to hurt, otherwise I'll never get to sleep tonight. Please, bright eyes, some magic, one more puncture wound.

I could get no love from humans, so I went to the forest to live amongst the trees. I fell in love with a poplar. So smooth and tall. So rich the sound its leaves made when it played the rushing wind like a celestial muse. But the tree did not return my amorous advances. Day after day, I was tortured by the silent beauty's indifference. The following spring, after the snow had melted, I cut the poplar down. I sawed its body into planks and beams and built a house out of it. Satisfied that I could control the form that had in the past daunted me, I lived inside for years until I finally grew weary of the view. I burnt the house to the ground and danced in the ashes. See the warning signs on the faces of the others. Listen to the stories they tell you about me. They aren't lying. I am that which beckons, then twists and brutally reduces. Look closely, can't you see my tail and claws? Can't you see the sharpened teeth, the way my pupils contract and my smile becomes unbelievably big when you approach? I never attempt to hide this ugliness yet all you see is the smile and the approachability. You are hopelessly attracted. I never plan on capturing your imagination and your undivided attention and then swallowing your mind whole. It is just what happens. I cannot claim intellectual superiority as mine. I possess no malicious intent as you might think months after our meeting. It is the vacancy of my life. The howling chasm of my existence that causes me to devour any sign of life that comes close enough for me to make contact with. I will mean no harm as I humiliate and belittle you. I will show no apparent concern that I have reduced you to a smoldering mound in front of your friends. They will not think any less of me after your demise. They'll remember me for the rest of their lives and forget your name in the next instant. If it makes you feel any better, I will do it to them the first chance I get with the same speed and effortless efficiency. The final irony is that you walk away feeling momentarily elated and then pathetic when in reality, I am the one who is pathetic. Pray for me as you hate yourself and the unceasing neediness of your life.

You are all colors. You are the birth of true jazz. You are ten thousand years of flowers blooming at once. You are the flavor of sunset. You are perfect like the stars that watch over me in the night sky of winter. I'm in a room with a mattress on the floor and little else. The rent is paid by washing dishes. I clean what they leave behind. I have enough to get by. I have no radio, no way to listen to music except to hear it through the walls from other rooms in the building. I don't read books because anyone who writes them must be oppressive and insecure. **YOU** If they really had something to say, they wouldn't feel the need to write it down. I only want to know about you. I have a picture of you that I cut out of a magazine. I look at it all the time. There is not the slightest trace of filth on your picture. Nights have passed unnoticed as I stare into your eyes. **CAN'T** Sometimes all I can think of is what a miracle it would be to kiss you and for you to want me to. Your unmoving face speaks to me. I close my eyes and can see your face clearly. I wonder what I would say if you told me to tell you everything. I never talk to people unless I want to get information from them or want to keep them at a distance. I use language as a shield. **BREAK** So much of what I do is an act. I act like a human. That's why I walk the streets as much as I can. I want to absorb as many human traits as possible so I can utilize them when the need arises. At work, I try to think of things that I could tell you. I have never talked to anyone because I wanted to know about them, or wanted them to know me. I have always spoken out of survival or fear. With women, I just repeated things I heard other people say. **A** I used catch phrases. I have never loved a woman. I have been with some but I never knew why. I just went through the motions. I don't know if it felt good or not. Afterwards, I would be silent, staring at the ceiling. They would ask if I was ok. I would reply with something I heard somewhere like, "Can't complain," or "It's Super Bowl Sunday!" They thought I was strange. They would always leave. I never cared. **WHORE**. It's different when I think of you, though. I never write anything down, because I think it's a waste of time. I know what I know. I don't need any information I can't use. If I forget something, then I didn't need to know it. The thought was obviously weak and my brain killed it off. I systematically go through my thoughts, sifting through the facts of my existence and the things that I use as deception to keep humans from knowing me. I want to know you. I want you to make me tell you everything about me. I want you to be the only person in the world who will ever know me. I want to hear you say that you want me. I want to feel your arms around me. I want to feel your heart beating against my chest and your breath on my neck. If you want me, you can have me. I have never kissed your picture. Out of respect, I never speak to it. I never take it out of the room. I don't love you. How can you love a piece of paper? Something that could be burned in a few seconds or thrown out and hauled away with tons of garbage. I just stare, prepare myself for our unlikely meeting and make sure I get to work on time.

The moon will never lie to anyone. Be like the moon. No one hates the moon or wants to kill it. The moon does not take anti-depressants and never gets sent to prison. The moon never shot a guy in the face and ran away. The moon has been around a long time and has never tried to rip anyone off. The moon does not care who you want to touch or what color you are. The moon treats everyone the same. The moon never tries to get in on the guest list or use your name to impress others. Be like the moon. When others insult and belittle in an attempt to elevate themselves, the moon sits passively and watches, never lowering itself to any-

thing that weak. The moon is beautiful and bright. It needs no makeup to look beautiful. The moon never shoves clouds out of its way so it can be seen. The moon needs not fame nor money to be powerful. The moon never asks you to go to war to defend it. Be like the moon. I trust you from my room. From here, we are tight. It is late and the lights are low. I am away from the world. Finally. Two flights of stairs, door double locked. From here, neither of us are the frustrated, ready to explode animals that others see when they pass us on the street. Our eyes are not wild and full of compressed hatred. The streets scream. The buildings howl as they support floor upon floor of sweating human lab experiments. It is no surprise to me that hardly anyone tells the truth about how they feel. The smart ones keep themselves to themselves for good reason. Why would you want to tell anyone anything that's dear to you? Even when you like them and want nothing more than to be closer than close to them? It's so painful to be next to someone you feel strongly about and know you can't say the things you want to. I have been in that hell many times and so have you. On that one, we're united. There's nothing like a small room and some music. If you're lucky enough to have that, you know what I mean. The late night soundtrack takes me away from the one-way strangers of the street and all becomes as it should. I used to like reality, until they screwed it up and cheapened it so badly. I used to defend reality until they shot so many people and crushed so many spirits that I could no longer stand to be part of it. They tried to break me. Of course, they failed. Johnny Hartman is tonight's late night soundtrack. He never got his due. I think of him singing his beautiful, sad alienation in a lounge somewhere until closing time and going back to a hotel room to chainsmoke himself to sleep. His voice lets me know that he was well acquainted with pain and late nights. He is dead but I know him well. He is part of my self-created reality. He comes here and fills the air with his songs and it's good to be alive. It's not a matter of being tough enough to take what they give out. I can hack it anytime around these parts, but only a fool would waste the time trying. What do you have to prove? It's hard to find anyone who's worth a second of your time or even the slightest bit of your truth. But from here we can do it. In this silent, understood relationship, I am glad you are here and hope for your well being. From this anonymous room, we don't have to dwell on the ordinary, grinding tasks that keep us alive and make us dull. Here in this moment we are beautiful, nocturnal creatures and our thoughts and words are jewels guarded by the moon.

Louis Jordan came home one night after playing and crawled into bed, next to his sleeping wife. A moment later she was stabbing him. He sustained a puncture wound an inch away from his heart that nearly killed him, deep slashes on his face and hands. The doctors were afraid that he would not be able to play his horn again. For a little while today, I hated you. I hated you for being so beautiful and real. I hated you for waking up at night to find your arms around me. I hated your honesty and the way you make people relax when you are around them. I hated you for loving me unconditionally. You have called me on years of cheap emotion and cruelty that came from my fears. When you look at me and smile, I no longer feel scared or feel the need to run out of the room gasping for air. You don't make me feel like life is a waste of time and that all you get is cold sweat, and dark moments in small rooms all over the world, spending time with other desperate characters who are tearing a path across the night skies of desolation. ***Promotional item. On loan from Warner Cablevision. Not for re-sale***. Could you believe I didn't know what to do with your slow, warm affection? Could you believe I was scared by your endless giving giving giving? It took me awhile not to feel threatened by your strength, that never shows off, never brags, but just nourishes and makes time stop. The feeling of hatred passed in the time it takes for an eye to blink and I realized I had to take care of myself because I belonged to someone. Someone is thinking of me right now. I never doubt it. I know you will always be there. Yeah, I'm in my room somewhere. It's freezing outside and I am exhausted. Too many things to do. Too many people to answer to all the time. From here, I think of you. My body is wracked in pain and I am burning with fever. ***Promotional item. On loan from Warner Cablevision. Not for re-sale***. A lot of men want a woman to mother them. They get with a woman and they regress to the point where you might think him incapable of taking care of himself. I don't want another mother. I want a woman. I want to rise to the occasion. I want to learn and bask in your glow. I want to protect you and do whatever I can to give you strength. There is no twist to this. I am not about to blow my brains out. You have not cut me up like others have. It's just this. I want to love you with everything in me. I need your help because I don't know anything about it. I am suspicious and ready to leave and hit the cold road for the frozen dawn. I am just going to trust you completely. I see now that it's the only reason to be here. After kissing you, I cannot remember what it was like to have kissed another woman. ***Promotional item. On loan from Warner Cablevision. Not for re-sale***. At this point I am not sure if I ever have.

I broke my body trying. You choked on your tongue laughing. I prepared and waited. You covered your fear of failure with cheap bravery and antagonism. I was your figure of fun. You were nothing to me at all. I was your joke. You were my lesson. I failed in your world without trying. You failed without knowing. The mask laughs. The mask pulls its mouth into a cruel, hideous mask of a mask. I was taken and gutted. This is appropriate behavior for the mask. The mask suddenly turns angry and I realize that the anger is because my face is not rendering the effects of the pain that is being inflicted. The mask is infuriated by my inability to die. It only hurts to a certain point and then it becomes my domain and I am in complete control. Yes, it hurts but my mind is clear and I am aware I am in pain and nothing worse can happen to me. The mask inflicts more pain but my facial expression changes only to let the mask understand that I know it is giving me all it has and I am taking it. It is the only thing I have talent for. Taking pain. It is my true calling. I am not sure if I earned this or if I was born with it so I never allowed myself to be too proud. By the time I realized that I was able to withstand long and steady seasons of pain, it was just a way of life. The mask is biting its lower lip in concentration. The mask has hit me with all it has and I'm still here. The mask turns away wordlessly and leaves me. I cannot tell if the mask's departure is out of frustration or respect. All I know is that I am still here and ready for more. It pays to be ready for pain and an alien to pleasure. Makes it easier to live with the way things are. You can only take me so low. After that it just doesn't hurt anymore. Your words and blows lose meaning and effect. You lose control of the situation. I can withstand any beating you can administer effortlessly but would die from receiving. How? I have waited. I have paid. I have scarred myself crawling through the guts of the machine, seeing how it works. You reward yourself with self congratulating accolades but you have not paid the price that must be exacted to know. I have been humbled and humiliated. I have felt the muscle pull away from the bone. For a time I was mislead into thinking that I avenge these acts of harm against me. I realized that by living and growing stronger on a diet of scar tissue, I had something better than revenge. I have the best of your bad situation. I am like the roach, the rock, the mountain. I will not die. I will not break. I will not move. Face it. You'll go to your grave knowing you never had what it took to stop me.

The doomed axe. Booker Little, Clifford Brown, Kenny Dorham, Bubber Miley, Lee Morgan, all alarmingly talented trumpet players. All died young. To survive it, you have to be a mean motherfucker like Miles. Three bodies are here with me in my room. I didn't kill them. I just knew them. It was not a good week. A musician friend slipped into a coma and passed away a few days ago. Yesterday I spent the morning getting questioned about the death of a friend where I was the only witness besides the killer. **CRITICS** Hours later I received a letter telling me that a young man I visited in the hospital had succumbed to leukemia. The mother thanked me and said that I gave the young man a lot to "ponder" after I had left his room. I guess life is sacred so you have to protect and value it? **JUST** I would never be a parent. What a con. You risk raising something that hopes for your death and hates you endlessly. Something that will start out unable to feed or clothe itself and then through your vigilant nurturing, will grow to become something that will insist you fucked it up. **PICK** Life is great. You can sit around in a room and think about dead people and what they could have been, if the life that drove them to the depths of pain and despair had not been brutally ripped away from them. **AT** I often think of the horror of my friend's last seconds alive. There must have been one clear millisecond where he knew he was going to be killed like a fact of life. Yeah, here's your fact of life: you're going to be shot in the face for absolutely no reason whatsoever. **SCABS**. You will never know the name of your killer, or what made him do it. You will never know how the lives of the people who knew you will be partially destroyed. How, on the anniversary of the night on which you were hastily dispatched, some people who knew you will sit in their rooms and stare at the floor and try to deal with it. **THEY** It makes me think about my last moments and wonder what they will be like. I wonder if I will die tragically and alone, spewing ancient, incoherent fury. **MAKE** Or perhaps I will die soft and content, somehow having extinguished memories of what I once was years ago. And why do I have it my mind that to be content is to have utterly failed? I guess I see contentment as finally giving in to the fruits of their paradise. **MY** Fruits with big price tags, laced with poison and rotten on the inside. It is why I set up adversarial relationships with anyone I deal with. Be it blatant or subtle, it is always there. **SCARS** It's honest and what humanity is all about. Why do we try to become close to another? To better understand and define ourselves and distance ourselves from our fear. So selfish. Muted survival of the ego through pickpocketing someone else's. I have tried to love and all it did was destabilize me. I felt swindled. **GROW** Like I had gone to the amusement park and went on one of the stupid rides and was mad when I was asked to get off. What was I thinking? What the hell was I after? What a waste of time. What a ridiculous human folly. I'd rather die in a shootout with no weapon. **STRONGER**. They're going to have to kill me a few times to make sure they got it done. A life without ingesting the usual amount of their toxins—I'll be pretty hard to bring down. I think in the final rounds, that will be the reason to get up in the morning. Just to survive them. Certainly not to love or hate them.

Winter is over, leaving me stranded on streets filled with loud strangers. Duke Ellington playing in my room. Library of Deconstruction. Profiles on the leveling of buildings. Nothing about what was built in their place. Lessons of hardness. Don't get

high—go get your nose broken. You'll learn more about the custom-tailored crisis that awaits you. USA. Microwaved cold warriors. As if in a dream, Willard looked into his eyes and saw an insanity that could soon be his own. "Colby..." The breathing, trembling few wait for the river to give the body back. He lugged a fifty pound sled of explosives through blizzards to blow up bridges. I go to the store. I fear only my desire for confrontation. The great mysteries: what she is doing right now and what she is thinking. Has she thought of you at all? Has she any plans of contacting you again? After letters sent to her and time spent thinking of her, she becomes more mysterious than the great pyramids. Thoughts of this mere human become more compelling and intriguing than anything else you can imagine. She has more power over you than the law. The idea of your death pales in comparison to what she is doing right now at this very moment. What you would pay to be able to see her and not be seen? What would you endure to know? Your curiosity and preoccupation with this infuriates you. You are being passively dominated. You have enslaved yourself. Your need shackles you to yourself. It's one thing to be humiliated by someone. But humiliating yourself alone in your room is self-inflicted pain on a different level. Ultimate. Beyond irony. You think of her before you go to sleep every night. In the dark you remember when she was right beside you. You have thought of her so much that she is more conceptual than actual. You wonder what occurs to her. How her mind works. How she could tell you the things she did and all of a sudden disappear. Sleep tight old friend. It's ok. As you breathe right now she's getting off with someone else and has no intention of ever seeing you again. If it makes you feel any better, there's a good chance that somewhere, some guy is already bored with her. Not likely.

I missed it before it was gone so I would be ready for the time when it left for real. I knew it was on its way out because it was made by human hands. Greed always shows itself early on. Most don't see. Too busy trying to make one of their own. If it's possible to mainline shadows, I will find the way. Because I want out. I don't hear the voices on the phone. There's nothing they say that I have to know. People are best on records and books because you can turn them off or put them back on the shelf. I prefer the crystallized moments of human artistic search than hearing on the news what acts of horror the idiots have committed. People try to talk to me on the streets. I have my filter up to make very sure I cannot understand them. I hear the attempt at language, which to them is just sounds strung together in a mindless stream. I tell them to go cure themselves. Yes, cure yourself. Shut up and cure yourself. Get over it. If you're going to beat yourself to death fine, but don't make me have to suffer your common stupidity. I tried to talk to one of them several weeks ago. It was like going to a movie. All of a sudden I was doing that warm-blooded-animal-stranded-in-a-city thing. I didn't believe a word that came out of either of our mouths. I felt like I was a great actor working with a neurotic script. A method actor so deep in the part that I actually became it. Pretty insane, right? I like the shadows these days. Luckily, the city I live in has lots of broken streets where fallen people live. This is where I walk. There are no bars for the idiots to crowd around and line up to get into. There are no clubs where you can wear your overpriced clothes and show off your hair. Just poorly lit, ruptured streets and sidewalks. And in this shadow world, I breathe in darkness like a vaccine.

70's bedside memo from Hughes inside a black-out curtained suite in Mexico. I always planned on an early retirement. I was right about it coming but I didn't expect it to be this soon. A loner, I have always been, but a recluse is the last thing I thought I would become. I sit in my small room with hardly anything in it. I wait for night to come so I can venture out. During the day it is too much. The stares and the continual bothering make it impossible to control my temper. I feel like lashing out at those who treat me like a prop for their amusement. It is, of course, my own fault. If you are good at what you do, don't let anyone know. They will only drain you and take everything they can and leave you dead on the floor. They will not notice that they are leeching your blood. All they know is their own desperation. If you aspire to be more than average, you will have to deal with the flak that inevitably comes when you mix with the multitudes. To be widely recognizable is a mistake. Anything you do to promote visibility brings you everything bad and you have no right to complain. It is your vanity, ego and pride that will get you in trouble every time. The smart man knows not to put trust in anything but numbers and the weakness of man. Better to fully understand and accept human nature and deal with people knowing that they are always thinking of themselves, even when they are at their most philanthropic. After all, acts of philanthropy are just expensively cloaked ways to demonstrate power. It is impossible for anyone to do acts of goodwill when they do not in some way, benefit themselves. You can rule out the concept of friendship early on and make sure you find ways to keep your associates paid and hungry for more. That way, they will, more often than not, be your "friends." Make sure they never know all the facts and don't hold all the pieces to the puzzle. In your absence they are capable of conspiring to take you out with their assembled bits of knowledge. It happens all the time. It happened to me. Good thing I'm too high to care.

The whitest white dipped in clinging dirt. Another summer has thrown its corpse on my floor. The streets have given birth to even more strangers. Rivers of urine stripe the sidewalks. It rained the other day and the only thing that occurred to me was it would wash the smell away for a few days. Tonight is the first hot night. Outside my window, the human noise factor is intense. It's past midnight. They talk too much. They scream liquor-fueled idiot chatter. I pull away and close the door. I think about how it's all going to play out. How much time people spend trying to get across to each other, trying to clear their names. Trying to overturn the charges brought against them. I have decided to tell them that it's all true and not seek a fair trial. It's the only way to be free. Stop trying to matter. I could get my body tattooed with air-colored ink and walk invisibly amongst them. I have heard people say that they felt closer to their parents after they have died. Maybe if I treat people as if they were dead, I could get along with them better. I want to be able to like living people somehow. As it is now, they're best coming through speakers or trapped between book covers. Here I go into the heat. Four months as a human anvil.

Why do people go to public places to be alone? Do they need witnesses? If you are sitting alone, feeling bad, are you wallowing in self-pity, or is it possible that things are bad for you and it's driving you so deeply into yourself that you forget what time it is, where you are and how to speak when spoken to? I have opened myself to ultimate vulnerability. Say anything, it no longer matters, no longer hurts. Call me all the names. Solipsistic, self-absorbed, cruel, ignorant, pig, dog, rat, snake, dirt. Nail my feet to the floor. Put a stake through my heart, a six foot spear through my head. You might have already. I'm not going to check. Nothing hurts and I am past caring about my appearance. Got a problem

with me? Get it all out. Empty yourself all the way. But when you're done, leave. I met a beautiful woman who spoke to me like no one had ever before. I listened but moved away because I did not trust her kindness. She pursued me. This filled me with confusion. I could not understand what she wanted with me. She told me she hoped that someday I would love her. All at once, I was overwhelmed by her honesty and bravery. I could never say something like that to anyone. It made me want to protect her forever. I was unable to walk away from her even when everything in me told me to leave. I saw that it was my cowardice, masked as scar tissue from my previous humiliating experiences, telling me to keep away. I decided to be brave as she had been and went to her. Time passed and I experienced feelings that startled me. She disappeared and left me with the taste of air. No word, no warning. I don't know where or for what reason. I thought of everything I did and said. At the end of all the thoughts, I came to the same conclusion—I must be a horrible person. So if that's what I am, I must do horrible things. I work hard at anything I put myself to. I work hard at being horrible and making a horrible life for myself. Isn't that what you're supposed to do when you're horrible? Be what you are, right? Well ok then. I got to work. Now I see it was my desperate loneliness masked as bravery that drew me to her. To know true ugliness is to know the truth of yourself. Many are spared this. It is hard for me to accept the fact that my achievements have merely been the exploitation of my accumulated failures, but I accept it because it's the truth. I see myself as an animal in need of animal things. Need for human kindness is something I attempt to conquer by falling below it, by fooling myself into believing I am too weak to contain its power. I created it all in my mind and can destroy it there as well. It is obvious to me that I cannot entertain such a concept without suffering. Why suffer? Why go out of your way to turn yourself into a victim who mainlines pity? No reason that I can see. I don't hate this woman. She obviously had her reasons for leaving. I'll just never get to know. Mystery is a combination of facts that are not apparent to you. It very well could be that the thing you want to know most in the world is a simple, well-worn fact to a man who just walked past your window. My curiosity is nothing more than one of vanity's many voices speaking to me as I try to go to sleep at night. I allow myself true love, a love that is invincible—I love music. I worship the pure miracle of music, not the motivation, the events or the ones who create it. To love humans, you must love humanity. To love a woman, you must love women. I cannot find the strength.

I could fall in love with a cruel desert that kills without passion, a canyon full of scorpions, one thousand blinding arctic storms, a century sealed in a cave, a river of molten salt flowing down my throat. But never with you. There was a house I spent time in many summers ago. A woman lived there. Imprisoned by her touch and mocking smile, time passed me. I did not want to leave. The longer I stayed, the weaker I became. The days passed and finally my self-hatred grew inside this beautiful house of paralysis, snapping me out of the coma of delusion I was in. All at once she was done with me and I was pushed out the door. Years later, the memories of the house and the woman inside haunt me when the weather grows warm. Broken dreams of conquest stabbed with failure. Of hope driven mad by emptiness. Of the long march that ends in muted defeat. Tricked by bad maps and dry river beds. Blood drying silently on stones under an unrelenting sun. All the time the truth was there trying to tell itself to me but I did not heed the warning. And through the years, she has risen out of heat driven mists like a cobra. Different faces, same killer. Yes, they are all the same. I learned the lesson after many self-inflicted deaths. I understood the truth after mutinous nights where my thoughts threatened to reduce me to nothing. It was a revelation. And now their masks fall away when they attempt to meet my eyes. Our conversations are automatic. They see that they have no control over the situation and have no default setting. There is at first a display of anger at their secret being revealed and then contempt because in order for me to know, I must have suffered the consequences of desire and desperation. Finally, the eyes narrow and a cold, mirthless reptilian smile creases the face with a million faces. A hiss emits from the mouth and the truth makes a wall between us.

I put cardboard up on my windows. I left small strips to look out onto the street. It's a paper thin barrier but it's like blinders for a horse. The less I see, the better. I figure it might cut down on sniper attack. I prefer artificial light to that of the sun. If I had my way, it would be night all the time, so I make my room perpetual night. At night, I am the only one alive. All the creatures outside are just extras in the movie. My face still hurts from the operation. I had tear duct implants placed inside my nasal cavity. All I have to do to make it look like I am crying is tilt my head forward, squint slightly and tears come rolling out of my eyes one after the other. I need the fake tears for my work. I'm an actor on the great urban stage. I have to get along with people, and since I can feel nothing for them, I had my tear glands removed years ago in a fit of youthful ignorance. I figured that crying was for weaklings, so fuck it. **GONNA DYE MY HAIR**. Now I can at least give the impression that I care. I can "cry" at movies, funerals and other moments where it is advantageous for me to feign feelings. **GONNA PIERCE MY FACE.** I have been taking acting classes as well. It's hard work. I can put on a good show when I have to. I do really good "concern" and my look of "understanding" is excellent, so says my instructor. **GONNA GET SOME TATTOOS**. The hardest was "fear." To look like you're "afraid" of something was beyond my comprehension for a long time. My instructor would stand in front of me and make these faces I found very funny. **GONNA WRITE A BOOK**. I asked him what the feeling of fear was like and he told me to imagine I was about to be murdered and "go with that emotion," We do that a lot. Well I remember being murdered and I didn't act like him. I was expressionless when it happened. Once I died, I decided to stay dead. I don't occupy places. I haunt them. When I'm by myself, I don't feel anything, I don't fear anything and I don't want for anyone. I spend time with women but it's only for practice. That's where the tear gland implants are an amazing asset. **GONNA TALK SOME SHIT**. We're at a table in a restaurant and she's telling me that her dog ran away when she was eight and how it still affects her to this day and right into my spaghetti, the tears come out. The look on her face is priceless, it saves me another trip to the acting coach. When I tell a story like that, I will use her facial expressions to get it across. **GONNA MAKE THE BIG BUCKS**. I look over at a guy at the table across from me and he subtly gestures towards his eyes and gives me the thumbs up—he knows I have the implants. Soon after hearing the dog story, I told it to another woman, used the tears and the facial expressions. He works it. He scores. There's nothing to fear. Stay dead baby.

I'll be all that's bad and you can be all that's good. Would that make you happy? You could be right all the time and I would be wrong all the time. The rules are not allowed to try and rehabilitate me in any way. You are not allowed to try to make me yours. You are not allowed to try to make me become like you. Can you deal with that? Save your breath. Parthenope calls me on the phone. She asks me how I am. I tell her that I am feeling better than she ever will. She doesn't get mad at the insult, she's used to this. She starts in again.

"I think you are a good person but you're misunderstood. *I* understand you. I am drawn to you. I hope this is not embarrassing you, but I cannot help the way I feel."

I tell her that I didn't hear what she said, could she say it again? She does in measured, slow speak. She wants me to hear every word. She says,

"I wish you would open up to me. I wish you would give me a chance. I am not like the others. I see you differently than they do."

I tell her the acting classes are doing some good but she has to get deeper into the part, she's not convincing me yet.

"More feeling, you stupid cow," I tell her.

This pisses her off.

"No wonder you live alone. With the way you are, you'll live alone for the rest of your life. I am ready to give you everything and all you can do is make fun of me and put me down. You're just showing me what a coward you are. If you were really as tough as you act, you wouldn't insult me so. You're afraid of real love. I am stronger than you'll ever be and you know it." I yawn.

"Probably." I reply. "That sounds good, we'll go with that one."

"You need me you son of a bitch. You motherfucker. You need me."

She's really mad now. I wait for her breathing to slow down and then ask her, "Is there anything else you wanted to talk about or was that it?"

I hear the phone smash against the wall and glass break. I hang up and take the CD of Black Sabbath's misunderstood masterpiece, *Sabbath Bloody Sabbath* off pause and resume my night.

The next day, I got a call from a friend who lives in her building. Apparently, she threw herself out of her window and died on the sidewalk. Her body was found on cinder blocks, head, tail and claws cut off, radio gone, torso covered in graffiti.

The sky turned a beautiful blue and the sun shone. My bank account filled with money and I got laid three times in a week by three females who never asked my name.

You can get what you want. Never sell out. Don't break. Don't weaken. Don't let the kindness of strangers be your salvation, for it is no salvation at all. Unless you sleep alone, you sleep with the enemy. Never come out of the storm. On the other hand, maybe *you* should. You don't have what it takes to go the hard way. Come out of the cold and sit by the fire. Let them warm you with smiles and the promise of friendship's fortune. Lose your edge. A soft body and a chained mind suit you. Chances are, you don't have what it takes to walk the frozen trail. Stay home and relax.

You should hear how beautiful the name I give you is when I look at you from across the room. The very thought of it is as wonderful as a planet covered with roses. I watch your mouth move as you speak to the man across the table. I imagine the interesting things that you are telling him. I think of all the things I would love to hear come out of your beautiful woman mouth . Striking intelligence, lightning humor. I think of the thrill of an intelligent woman talking just to me. I put eyes in your head. Eyes that could lead armies off cliffs, horses and all. This is why I come from no place and go home to no one. This is why I walk the streets alone, searching for nothing, everything. Street level magic. You'll never know that just sitting across a room full of people, I have transformed you into a goddess. A destroyer of despair. The answer to a shipwrecked, stranded prayer. I see people sitting in bars, looking out the window at me. I look away because I feel like they know I don't belong. They look so natural looking into the street, looking at the world from coffee houses, watching me as I move. **I WOULD BE A SCIENTIST**. Always moving. I never go in. I know that if I set foot into such a place, the people in it would yell and throw things and I would be tossed out. I don't want to go in places like that anyway. I don't want to sit next to people and listen to them talk. I don't want them to talk to me. I don't want to smell them. I don't want them to touch me. I see them on the street and I look at their hair and the clothes they wear. I tell myself that we all had mothers. We were all born. How did I turn out so different than all of them? Why do I have absolutely no idea of what their world is? Why do I feel that a lot of the time I am trespassing? They act like the streets and the buildings and everything else were built especially for them. I feel strange everywhere I go when they are around. Their presence reminds me that there is not much room for me in the world. I have known this fact for a long time so I have dealt with it. **I WOULD CLONE ROSIE O'DONNELL, JENNY McCARTHY AND RUSH LIMBAUGH, MILLIONS AND MILLIONS OF TIMES**. I walk the streets in places where people speak different languages and don't look at me when I pass. I return to a small room and live alone, quietly. The thing I notice about them is that they don't seem aware of what's around them. It's like shoes that fit so well you forget you have them on. They do not seem ready. **PLACE THE INFANTS IN THE ARMS OF LOVING CHRISTIAN FAMILIES**. They do not seem ready for anything to befall them. I on the other hand, am aware of everything. I can hear buildings lean. I feel the glow of street lights. When people pass me in the street, I can smell the blood underneath their skin. I can hear the sun rise. In my room, I sit on the floor and read magazines I found on the sidewalk that homeless men had tried to sell and left behind. I read old magazines about movie stars and their lives. They are smiling and looking at the camera. They were born to smile into machines that were made to capture and document their happiness for others to witness. I am a criminal loner in their world. I'm an ugly spotted animal who stands at the far end of the water hole and drinks where it's shallow and teeming with insect larvae. From looking at the pictures on the garbage-stained pages, I know one thing: these people are not ready. I am ready. **GET IN MY SPACE SHIP AND BLAST OFF**. I sleep on a stack of cardboard and old blankets. I wait for nothing. I hope for nothing. I love nothing. I forget as many things as I can, so my mind will be empty as possible—ready. I fear nothing because I am so aware of fear, that I am fear itself. **I WOULD BE THAT LAUGHING SPECK ON MARS**. I don't know where they're going in busses or cabs. I don't know what the message of their laughter is. I don't know why they touch. I only know about being ready. I only know the broken sidewalks and the smell of cheap food coming out of doorways and flat faced men sitting on porches, drinking out of bottles wrapped in paper bags. I can walk on the edge of their world almost unnoticed. They buy ten pairs of shoes. They insulate themselves from pain with laughter, with alcohol, with drugs, with movies. They think they are ready. They make plans to go the next comfortable place where there will be smiling people and laughter waiting for them. But they are not ready.

Another night. The temperature is flesh. The moisture in the air is a poor man's sauna. And on a night like this, you must have music. To my rescue comes Gene Chandler singing the "Duke of Earl." The music hangs in the air so righteously. These moments make life bearable. People don't mind their business enough for my liking. All that talk from nowhere. Zero substance. Their experience knows the bounds of a postage stamp. Yet they tell you how it is and how it's going to be. I have erased myself. My past is passed. People I knew are dim memories. Few faces, names or events exist in my mind. Now it is night. Summer. I do not remember the nights of my youth. I look at young people on the streets and wonder if I was ever like that. I wonder what they are thinking and if I have ever thought their thoughts. Walking down this street, now that they have left, the silence has allowed my other senses to explore. Moths make furious attacks at the street lights. The choir of insects is symphonic and seems to hang suspended in the air's moisture. The smell of foliage makes the darkness full of life. So strong that you can turn your back on it and take it for granted. You don't have to remember it because it is a constant. Somehow truer than fact. One of the few memories I have is of having a memory that held every thought, every feeling, perspective and perception I ever had captive. I vaguely remember that I was always angry, sad or in some kind of need. I do not remember the moment nor the events that lead to the systematic erasure of my memory and associations with people. Now the seasons pass by me like a breeze through thin curtains. I remember no names when I am introduced. I don't even know my own name or if I had one. I'm sure I did but like every other fact on this planet—it doesn't matter.

My flag is the color of late night ceiling. On my flag are stars. They have all blown their brains out. Their shattered brilliance is scattered all over the worn cloth. In my removed from the world room, I am glad you are there, veteran. I am glad to know you are in a room somewhere armed and silently bleeding. It is good to know that you know that no one will understand you. No one will know your wordless panic and empty stepping, slow moving desperation. You are alone but not alone. You are crowded in with people who are alive yet who have not lived. When they reach out to you, their well-meaning arms are but amputated stumps. Their concern is mutilated with guilt and is limited to the confines of their tiny lives. You have been cast adrift in a sea of humanity and are stranded invisibly. You are not alone. My fist hit the wall as yours did tonight. My phone did not ring as yours did not. The scars of my knowledge and regret are rising off my flesh as yours are. I know you're out there in my night as I am out there in yours. Doesn't matter if you've seen war or not. There are many ways to see too much. Experience comes back around to trap you in its claustrophobic, vast abyss. Those who want to be close only make you feel threatened. You like them, so you don't want them to get a glimpse of the horrific clarity with which you perceive. How you see the end of the story at the beginning and go along with it anyway until the pain becomes so all-consuming that all you can do is sit alone and wait for it to pass. When you live as a warrior, you don't think that dying as one would take this long and be dragged out with such agonizing, dishonorable tameness. The minutes alive humiliate. The days mock and the voices fill you with rage. Wear it silently and walk on. Keep moving up the trail. Stay inside the treeline and never give yourself up because the natives are grotesque in their friendliness. They will kill you and you will go out worthless. Alone is the only way to walk the line and you know it.

Cool. Cool. Cooler than one hundred Japanese punk rock girls walking unsteadily in their hilarious stack heel silver knee-high boots, spending their meaningless money in clothes stores. I am imagining how great it would be to be able to disintegrate at will. Not disappear in the blink of an eye, but fade into grey, into nothing in the space of a minute. The memory of me would fade in the people who I was just in front of. They would all of a sudden not know why they were standing there. I would like to be able to gently drift in and out of existence when I wanted to. I don't want to kill myself. I still want to listen to Charlie Parker and sit in a room alone at four in the morning. There are moments to live for. There are times, hours slammed together, that are definitely worthwhile. It's all the other hours, minutes and unendurable expanses of time that drag me by my collarbone slowly through the mindlessness of their blank words. Their culture is an amazing patchwork castle of latex and plastic. The edges have been rubberized and the colors have been enhanced. For the monotonous seas that they force me to sail across, I would like to be null and void. Not isolated, but stagnant and floating in zero light heavy syrup like a canned peach. Like a bottle of desert wind captured at night. Why do I want for this? Because I am devoid of anger towards man. No living human is worth my love or hate. No matter how horrible someone may be, no matter how hideous their deeds—I have much in common with them. I accept this totally, but I cannot accept them at all. I am no longer flexible like a new blade of grass in the wind. My surface is hardened and unresponsive to subtle climatic changes. My thoughts are not agitated, but too tired for tolerance. My synapses are gnarled and thick with scar tissue. The only thing I respond to is the old voices. The brave human toned signal I medicate myself with in my room. The long-dead greats allow me to endure the moronic hammer of existence. I am too far gone to be rehabilitated. What good would rehabilitation be for me? It took me years to dull the blathering roar. Why bring back my ability to hear their watered down money mantras? Your genitalia has been overworked and overexposed. Your beats are beat. Your dances are listless and robotic. Your cities are corruption in motion. You don't consume—you loot and ransack. Sales are nothing but low-level feeding frenzies. The desperation hides behind makeup, hair care products, implanted cosmetic aids and taste-fucked-out-of-mouth clothing. You're an almost corpse. An "also-ran" who has run aground. You're given to the chance to dress up and parade yourself through the ruins of the crumbling tombs of long gone inspiration. Don't ever wonder why there will never be another horn player who sounds like heaven or another dancer who makes you feel your guts, or another writer who will inspire you to rip the sunglasses from your eyes and see it. There's no more to see. No more music to face. That's why I want to be able to fade out. I want to deaden my clarity. Horror jolts me when I look at one of you and see a pair of beautiful eyes that make me think your mind might contain a world that could hold me as the bolts shake loose and fly from my frame. No. I want to be sand under your feet when that happens. The crushing pain when I discover your hollowness is too much.

Mistakes. Not knowing when you're not wanted. Not getting the hint, the shove, the brush off. Forgetting that the facts don't change. Coming back and getting what you deserve for being so stupid. Not learning from that and going back again. Thinking that at some point they won't turn on you like they do on all the others. Sticking around too long. These are some of the great mistakes. Master your ego, and you own your destiny. It can be found. It is somewhere in the night. It is lurking past midnight and you have to be alone to be able to find it. You can be absolutely sure that you will not find it in company, no matter how intimate it is. The darkness on the edge of town can only be articulated alone.

In the black heat of this summer night, I have found it. The beautiful, sonorous pitch of exquisite loneliness. Not saddening. Not alienating. It is friendly and lets you know that you have been, are and will be.

Right now, I am alone with my memories and the sound of my breathing. Traffic sounds have died down. My mind is full of tree lined streets and the sound of thousands of insects. All the burnt nights, all the wasted time, the humiliation and failure of my life cannot take these images away from me.

And what is the "It"? Your true self. You. The one who comes out when the coast is clear. The one who cannot stand up to scrutiny. The one that is so pure that it cannot defend itself. It knows nothing other than itself. It is only understood by one. The one outside the window at night when you are with someone. It is as close to perfection as you will ever come. It is the one who keeps us ever so slightly apart.

It is now I can think of my invisible family. The dead and unknown. Those who feel what I feel. I never meet them. I don't want to talk about this with anyone. Ever.

They smiled at me and told me everything was going to be alright. Then they tightened down the clamps that held my head still. The first blow of the hammer hit above one of my eyes and then I passed out or died. When I could open my eyes again, I saw that all my internal organs were nailed to the wall. I was still tied down to the floor but my head had been released from the clamps. That's how I was left. Alive, but emptied and uglified. I got out of the restraints and put myself together again. I am not bitter about it. Maybe I won't get disemboweled next time. I am trying. If I believed in a higher power, I would tell it. I would say something like, "Lord, I am trying to be good and I am trying to like people. I know that everyone is doing the best they can. I will try to do better." Instead, I just tell myself to be a good person. I work at it. I am not strong enough to maintain it. I am, for the most part, failing. There are moments where I triumph. I stood in front of the woman with the bad breath as she told me the same thing three times. I did not run away. I did not say, "Your breath is disgusting." I stood there like a stuffed animal and took it. I did not attack the man who chased me on his bike trying to take my picture today either. I kept my head down and walked to work. I was polite to the drunk soldier who followed me for two blocks shaking my hand every five paces, telling me the same thing over and over. I did not ask, “Could you please stop saying the same thing over and over to me while you exhale your stinking beer breath in my face? Could you stop holding my hand?” But he’s doing the best he can, right? Just like me. I should take that into consideration. There are the times when I am not strong enough. Someone smiles at me and my face freezes blank and my eyes go to the ground. Someone calls after me on the street and I hear them plain as day but I pretend I don’t and just keep walking. I get tired of stopping when I want to go. I get tired of talking when I want to be silent. I get tired of answering endless questions and tired of the petty abuse for which I have no recourse. I try to be good, hoping that maybe they’ll give me a sliver of space to exist in outside of this room. An insect-sized space where they won’t invade and take everything away. I want for this because I just don’t have what it takes to keep taking it day after day. Liking people is the hardest thing I have ever tried to do. I am not cutting it. I feel myself slipping.

I am turning invisible again. Running through the jungle into the hole. Becoming nothing. Where else can I go except into the darkness that silently curses me? When in doubt, become nothing. When my life rejects me, I become less and less until the pain leaves. I live in the cracks. I do not wait. I do not hope. I have no thoughts of breaking through to the other side. There is no other side. For me, there is only down. Down where nothing hurts. Down where nothing is cold. Down where they do not speak. I am tired of your human signal. The only sound I hear is my breathing and the scathing malice of the darkness. I am going to be executed by electrocution. I go to the chair willingly. The priest asks me if I have any last words. I shake my head no and thank him for his concern. I tell him I would like to talk to you before I die. You are brought in from behind the glass. I take your hand and put it on my heart so you can feel it beating. I whisper something in your ear. I walk back to the chair and calmly sit down. In a few moments, flames are sprouting from my head like, like, like flames sprouting from my head. I am dead. People rush over to you and ask what it was that I said but you never tell them.

Deny the beauty and turn the world ugly. Take non-control. Eliminate their options by cutting off your hands. Torture yourself so they cannot. Leave them no part of yourself that has not been ruined and only then will you be free. An attractive model in a tight, revealing skirt walks into a room full of men. She walks by them, trying to catch their eye. Usually, it's all she can do to avoid men looking at her. She gets frustrated when none of them will pay attention to her. She takes her blouse off, exposing her breasts. She throws the blouse up in the air and it lands on a man's shoulder. He brushes it off without looking up. All at once, the men simultaneously open books and start reading avidly. Somewhere, someone isn't impressed by your looks. Not all men jump through the hoops of your fire. You're unbelievably boring to more people than you'll ever know. Video music refugee.

Imagine a man dyeing his hair blonde after forty. The rockstar on his happy marriage to the model half his age, "I won't be sticking my banana in anyone's fruit bowl any longer." You look out the window of the plane you're flying in and think to yourself that in seven hours you'll still be in this seat. You imagine Rod Stewart tied to the wing of the plane waving at you frantically. No one on the flight can see him except for you. You wave a banana at him and smile. If everybody got what they wanted every time they wanted it, you wouldn't be alive to read this. If you think for a minute that any of these freaks are your friends, you're fooling yourself. The only ones I trust are criminals.

I'd like to borrow your morals for the weekend. *The song's dead as far as I'm concerned*, he thought to himself. He used to play it over and over in his head as he lay in his bunk. The song reminded him of her. He used to think of her all the time. It was the only thing that kept him going in prison. Life with no chance of parole. He thought of her. He thought of killing himself. She had written to say she had been married for three months but didn't have the heart to tell him until now; she hoped that it was ok and that he was happy for her. He threw the song out of his mind. Imagine being in prison for the rest of your life. Never getting out of there. Imagine if your line was, "I'm never getting out of here." Imagine life in prison when you're only twenty-two when you go in. Ever had a song that kept you strong in your mind? You go back and play it, but it no longer works. I feel good when that happens. It means I'm stronger than the situation that made me rely on the song for support in the first place. Songs that mend your broken heart. Everyone has one. They're the best ones to laugh at when you're over it. For me, nothing works. I know too much. I don't fool myself.

Someday you'll bake like I bake. You haven't thought about the dollar bill in your pocket for almost three hours. Why would you? It's mixed in with a few other dollar bills that were in there this morning. It was part of the change that you got back after you bought the paper. The man who gave the dollar to the man at the newsstand killed a woman two and a half years ago. She was jogging on the bike path in Rock Creek Park, Washington DC, early in the morning. He was sitting against a tree in a running suit, pretending to be stretching, and when she ran by, he ran after her, clubbed her to death and threw her in a recess by the creek. She wasn't found for fourteen hours. There were no witnesses and no suspects. He thinks about it from time to time but it doesn't register as anything much. It's just something he did, like a lot of things he did. And now a little of him rides with you.

No! You live through it! I don't give a fuck about you. No, I'm not looking at you. I'm not undressing you with my eyes. I don't think about what you might look like naked. I would prefer it if you kept your clothes on. I'm not a rapist. I never touched a woman who didn't want me to. I don't think about what sex with you would be like. I don't want to know your name. I don't want to have anything to do with you. I don't want to go to prison for something I didn't do. I walk way around you on the street. I purposely look away as soon as I see you. I don't want you to get the wrong idea and yell rape. At restaurants, I walk way around you with my hands at my sides, palms on my legs. I don't smile at you. I don't answer when you ask me something. I don't want you to say that I was sexually harassing you. I don't want you to have anything that could possibly used against me in a court of law. I will never get married. I don't want to pay someone every month for the rest of my life. I don't trust you. I'm not your enemy. You have nothing to fear when I'm around. All I'll try to do is get away from you as quickly as possible. I don't want to hurt anyone. I am not your friend. You don't know me. You will never know me. Fuck you.

I'd rather be vaguely despised, than weak like you. I don't give a fuck what your sexual preference is. The topic could not be more boring to me. I don't give a fuck if you like to fuck members of your own sex. I think the topic of paint drying is more interesting. You're here, you're queer—I'm bored already. Garbage is filling the streets. The country's literacy rate is falling like a stone, and I have to take time out to be reminded that you like to fuck a guy in the ass? Could you believe that some people don't care what you fuck as long as both parties agree? Could you believe that I think you're pathetic when I see you marching with your flags when the KKK still exists? I'm not homophobic. I'm just as interested in your sex life as I'm interested in staring at a bucket of dirt for thirty years. I'm falling asleep already. I bet it makes you mad that you're all the same to me. Straight. Gay. Bi. You're all the same. Boring. Nineteen piercings in your cock? Like to get tied up and beaten by some woman in black leather? Zzzzzzzzzzz.

I've got nerves that jingle jangle jingle. He nearly got hit by a fucking car while crossing 2nd Avenue. He was thinking about what he heard the whore say to the man in the doorway of that apartment building he just walked past. "She came back and she had a black eye. She was with this guy and he beat her up. All the time I thought she was out having a good time." He looked up and saw the headlights and the hood go down violently as the driver slammed on the brakes. The man in the cab stood on his horn the entire time it took him to stagger back to the curb and lean on the light pole. His heart was beating fast but the rest of his senses were dull and ringing. Truth was, he didn't give a fuck about what the whore said to the guy and he didn't really think he was going to die by getting hit by a car. So he stood there and waited for the light to turn green. He didn't belong to anyone. He looked at the couple embracing to his left. He wondered what they thought of each other. Maybe they each thought that the other one was the best thing that had ever happened to them. Maybe they made life bearable for each other so they went along with it in spite of the fact that the relationship had cooled months ago. *No one in the world for me* he thought to himself. *I belong to no one and no one belongs to me*. It's a big place and there's lots of people and he couldn't find anyone. He passed through the night as silently as he always did. Without protest. On the way back to his room he saw the old man that was always standing in the doorway of the building next to his. The old man was looking at the whores sitting on car hoods across the street. You can live a long time in silence and no one will get in your way. No one will come into your room, tell you to snap out of it and lend you a hand in getting your hammered mind back together. You can scream in silence for sixty years, die in a single room with no heat and not a single car will stop in your honor. No movies will be made about your life. Nothing will happen. It's an option.

You and me, nothing but a memory. Nothing but a closed history book. Nothing but a man swinging from a beam in the attic, dead thirty-eight minutes. You are something. I am something. You and me are nothing at all. We are extinct. I wish men weren't so fucking weak. You make me look bad. I have to answer for all the bullshit you get up to. I have to endure women saying shit like, "Oh, there's so much testosterone in the air," when she sees some men fixing a car. I hate it when men go to strip bars. It lowers the rest of us that know if a man has to pay to see a woman naked, he is a loser and probably should get weeded out. I hate having to be put in the same category as with these pieces of shit that wouldn't make it in the jungle. Little boys in men's bodies. No wonder women hate them. I do too. Fuck it. I hate all of you. People are disgusting.

They shoot whores, don't they? What about a little shack at the edge of the world? I could get a place at the last outpost. Live for years and never see anyone. I would have to hunt for my food. It would take years to detox civilization from my mind but eventually it would happen. What would my thoughts be of? A mind clear of the paranoia of crime and violence. No jealousy, no dread. Might be boring, but that would fade away as the years go on. No, it would never work. I'm addicted to fear and bad air. Without the threat of violence, I am nothing. Classic. The victim thinks he's the lucky one. Without too much noise and pollution, I get bored and depressed. Fuck it. I'm a typical contemporary case. Soon comes the breakdown and eventual betrayal. I have so much lower to go. I bet I have not yet begun to explore the depths of self-disgust. Wow. Something to look forward to. I could make a "Disgustumentary."

I have been living in the desert for quite some time. I got sick of the cities and the freaks they make out of people. No people out here. No people—no people problems. You get addicted to the rituals of decadence and fear. What is wrong with the system becomes what's wrong with you. You don't figure it out until you have eaten yourself alive. This afternoon, a woman came up to the front of my cabin. She said that she was magic and she would grant me a wish. I told her I didn't believe that she possessed such powers. She told me to hold out my hand and think of something I want that would fit in my outstretched palm. I did. The ring I had lost fifteen years ago appeared in my hand. I told her I was ready to make my wish. I wished that she turn into a grain of sand and throw herself into the wind. I threw the ring away, too. I want nothing more than to leave a clean slate for Death. I want no shadows to obscure the path when it's time to get taken out. Even if it's tomorrow. Too much time is spent wondering about what is to be. Too much time is spent trying to gain the approval of others. Who am I living for? All this time living for others while others are living for others. Does anyone ever live for themselves? Maybe people in prison. Maybe old people living in single, dimly lit rooms. People who have been discarded, thrown away and forgotten. People who know it all means nothing and have nothing to prove. They know it's all an act. No sell out. All the others are running desperately for approval. Me? I'm probably one of the worst. I am weaning myself away from them as best I can. I go on long spells of solitude and treat it like endurance training. A week, then a month. Soon longer periods will pass and I won't even notice. I will no longer feel the need to communicate. Those who feel the need to tell others things all the time obviously have problems facing themselves. Anyone with something to prove is insecure. Believe me on this one.

Things are going to be different. The sooner I get used to it the better. That's where they fuck up. They make the mistake of holding on. They think that they'll be able to hold out and not give into the shit building up around them. They try to bring their old ways forward with them. They get chewed up. You can't think that the pigs are going to be able to handle truth. I hate the idea of old fashioned morals and ethics. Hanging on to what was—living in the dark with the lights on. Personal pride seems to be a thing of the past. It's ok to be a weak piece of shit. Men especially. I think men should start acting more like the awesome beings that they are, instead of what I see all the time. It's hard not to be pathetic in modern civilization. It's almost a miracle not to get compromised in your sleep. The more I see men, the more I hate them. It's hard to conduct myself in an honorable manner. Why be honorable to weaklings and brainless scum? I am pulling away from civilization. I figure I have a few more years with this shit and then I'm gone. I won't miss it either. Only an idiot would get addicted to what's out there. You can dress it up as well as you can but I'll always see through it. Not enough samurai in the world today. Just a bunch of assholes running wild with much too much freedom. There will be no more protest music. There will be no more geniuses, no more greatness. It's over with. It will be just one fake out after another. More reasons to never go outside again. Poison death rays and uninspired fakes. You can't fool me. You can't tell me it's great. I'll just laugh in your face and charge you double for wasting my time.

Before I die I want to see Dolf Lundgren and Sylvester Stallone getting it on. Oh yeah. He started mailing her parts of his body. The idea started when he had to get a wisdom tooth pulled. Naturally, he asked to save the tooth. When he got home, he examined it. It was huge in his hand. He couldn't believe that thing came out of his head. He almost felt proud that he had a gap in the back of his head now. He thought of what he could do with this tooth, this trophy from his body. If he gave it to someone, it would really be saying something, now wouldn't it? Sure it would. It's not every day that someone gives you a body part. There was a woman he had been wanting to get close to for several months. He had tried writing her and calling her and she was friendly but every time he asked her out she made up some excuse as to why she couldn't make it. She had no interest in him besides a distant friendship. But like a fool, he kept hanging on to the hope that she would see he was sincere and the man for her. He figured you had to keep hammering away. He didn't understand that some people just don't want to know you and you should get the hint and move on without disgracing yourself. He wrote her a letter and sent her the tooth. He figured that would impress her greatly. After he mailed it he looked over the pamphlet the dentist had given him about wisdom teeth. He read a section that said wisdom teeth were useless and often came in crooked since there was no room for them in the jaw. The teeth were holdovers from the days when we had longer jawbones and it's not a bad idea to get them all removed. It was at this time that he came up with his master idea. He would go to the dentist every Friday and have a wisdom tooth removed. He would send it to her. She would be impressed as the tooth toll rose. The weeks went by and the teeth kept coming to her. She didn't mind the letters and occasional calls. He was an alright guy. Not the type for her but still he was alright. The weekly tooth bit quickly convinced her that he was fucked up and in need of help. Of course, she didn't respond. A quick note saying something like, "Stop sending me your goddamn teeth, you fucking psycho," would have been fine. He would have understood. He took her no reply to mean that she was warming up to him. A week later, he sent her the tip of the little finger on his left hand. It hurt like hell and it made him vomit when he did it, but he did it. Love is like that, so they say. The next week another letter and the tip of his left earlobe came to her. He got no reply. He stopped writing her and stopped sending her his body parts. It became clear that she wasn't interested in him. He grew his hair out to conceal the lost bit of ear and no one seemed to notice the missing bit of finger. Eventually he stopped thinking about her altogether. He went on with his life. All the love songs are wrong. You were stupid. No man or woman is worth it. Free yourself from the chains of dependency and betrayal. Stop making yourself into a pathetic slob. Never belittle yourself. Don't waste your time on people. If you can conquer your loneliness and master yourself, you will never have to be compromised by one of them.

Come on Schwarzenegger, gimmie that butt meat. Come one and rock my world cowboy. Oh yeah. I'm glad I found out before it was too late. These fucking breeders are so weak. All the great ones are dead. I listen to dead musicians. I watch dead actors on movie screens. I don't care about what any of these fucking breathers are doing. Wigs, buttplugs. I don't want to fuck any of them, befriend any of them, kill any of them. I reject it all. Modern culture, all their ways of life. None of them impress me. At the end of the day, they always roll over and become the bullshit they said they never would. So scared. They practice politics they don't believe in so no one will bring the witch hunt down on them. Men have become emasculated to the point to where they're just cowering nothings or idiotic rape machines. Don't pretend that you know me. You don't know shit about me. Your gods are weak. Your culture is weak. Your music, art, politics, lifestyle are all weak. You won't possibly die off fast enough for my liking.

Portrait of a fool painted with a knife. I disgust myself when I think of the pathetic things I've done to make contact with a woman. I want to punish myself for thinking that I could ever do it in the first place. Who the hell did I think I was? The truth is, every time I've compromised myself is because I took time out to try to get across to a woman. Usually I'm ok on my own. I don't disgust myself too often. Some of the letters I've written make me want to cut my hands off. I let my guard down. I paid the price every time. I have done my time with it. I should have learned my lesson the first time but like the fool I am I didn't. When I am alone, I don't hate myself. When I am with a woman, I know it's just a matter of time before I get ripped apart. A lot of men feel this way but they don't have the guts to say it out loud, they're afraid of being politically incorrect. They're afraid of some liar telling them they're insensitive and stupid. I say whatever the fuck I want. Your weak morality could never hold me anyway. Truth has always angered you. You watch, more men will avoid women as time goes on and your weak society crumbles at your feet. The sexes will grow further apart. Not all men like to stand around and be told they're rapists. They will become paranoid and further withdrawn. Rape and aggravated assault will become more common. Of course, I will have no part in this, as I would never do any of these things. You will never have me to blame for the terrible things that happened in your life. I'm one of the aliens who walked away from your fucked reality a long time ago.

Breathing meat. Aliens don't mix with people. You know you're a stranger when you go out for walks just to be around them. Thinking that someone will be out there for a magic rendezvous. You look in windows of bars to see if there's anyone in there waiting for you. I can fool myself over and over, walking amongst them. Long ago, I gave up on the idea of making contact with anyone. I look at people now like they are on display in a museum. They have nothing to do with me and I'm not part of their world either.

Humanity in my fist. They can all kiss my ass because I know that at the end of the day, it's all the same thing. They can talk a lot of shit but they still want the same thing. All these people who say they're politically correct are liars. All men still want the same thing and so do the women. They don't have the guts to stand up and say what they want. So fuck them all. If they don't like me, they can go get fucked. I know why Kurtz went up river. He was tired of all the weak fucks that populate the streets of every city in the world.

In the movie, she turned into three cobras. Three! Must have been one hell of a woman. Come closer so I can abuse you. It's in my blood. I'm good at two things. Taking and giving abuse. I'd rather give then receive. I get inspired all the time. I can't help myself. I can't talk to you for too long before I'm ripping on your shit. I try to restrain myself but sometimes it's overwhelming. It's not that I see something wrong with you. I just don't like people. I see all the bad examples. Even the good ones piss me off at this point.

Clear water on clean cloth. For a little while nothing is broken. Nothing horrible is about to happen. The driver is not asleep. His car's not sliding towards the concrete and steel median divider.

There will be no horrible phone call at a bad hour by an understanding highway trooper to a young man standing in the dormitory hallway in his underwear. "Are you Malone? Some cop is on the phone for you."

In moments like these when all things seem to be going well, I always have a sense of doom. Like it's too good to be happening. I used to live in a house by the beach. The nights were cool and the days were hot and long. The house had clean wood floors. I could have lived there for the rest of my life. At times I would stand in the living room and look over the place and think to myself that life couldn't be this good. There had to be a catch. There was. Months later as I was cleaning my friend's blood off the front porch after he had been shot in the head, I knew that there was always a catch, always a price to be paid.

When I was young, I would go visit my father at his house on the weekends. He would drill me with lessons I would surely need in later life. One morning it was fighting practice again. My father stood in front of me, put his hands in front of his face and told me to "Put 'em up!" and I would punch at his palms. Without warning, he swept one hand down and hit me in the stomach. He taught me to block my face and my front. This morning he did that and then he hit me between the legs hard. I felt life start slipping away. I had never felt anything like that before in my life. I asked him why he did that and he said, "Hit 'em in the face, hit 'em in the eye, make 'em hurt, make'em cry. Kick 'em in the balls."

That morning he decided I was ready to fight. He took me up the street to a house where there was a boy about my size playing in the yard. He looked at the boy and looked at me and said, "Do you see that kid?" I nodded. "Go get him." I was afraid of what would happen if I did but I was more afraid of my father. I went in and the boy stood up and said hello. I did the same and then I punched him in the face as hard as I could. The boy went running and screaming through a gate to the backyard. I ran out the front gate back to my father. He was standing on the sidewalk laughing so hard tears were falling from his eyes. His cigar ashes were all over his boots. "You did good, kid!" he said to me and slapped me on the back. He took me back to the house and I tasted scotch and bourbon and beer. He told me they were an acquired taste and I would like them later on.

Somehow I became a friend of the boy I hit. I don't remember how. I can't figure out why he would want to be my friend after what I did to him. It turned out that I was younger than he was. The fact that I had beaten him up always gave me superiority over him even in later years when he was a head taller than I was. I liked his family better than mine. I would escape my father's place on Saturdays and go over to his house to be with his sister and his mother and father. The boy's father had gone to college with my father. They were so different. I was scared of my father but I wasn't scared of his. The boy's mother was nice too, nicer than mine. Not crazy and hysterical. Sometimes I would spend the whole day over there. It was the only time I would see a mother and father together. Mine had been divorced before I could remember.

Many years later, I was fourteen years old and going to a prep school in the suburbs. My father called me one night and told me the family had driven the boy out to his first semester at college in Minnesota. The whole family had piled into the station wagon and driven to Minneapolis. The boy had been dropped off and the sister, mother and father had started their long drive back east. Around dawn, the father had fallen asleep at the wheel and driven the car into the median strip and been killed. The boy's sister had two broken legs and his mother was in traction.

I wore my uniform home from school that afternoon and got off the bus near the old neighborhood. I stopped in at the drug store and bought a comb and did the best I could to look neat.

I walked down the old sidewalk until I stood in front of their house. I walked up to the door and rang the door bell. I was let in by the boy's sister, who was on crutches. I introduced myself and reminded her that I used to live down the street and all. It was as if she wasn't listening or didn't care. She looked down and nodded her head and then swung it in the direction of her mother, who was in a bed in the living room in full traction. The mother remembered me and thanked me for coming. She told me that my father had called her.

The living room had not changed much. The piano was still by the front door and the room had the same smell as I remembered but it was all different. It was familiar but something had been ruined. It was as if the place had been ransacked yet nothing had been broken or moved. I remember the light was sharp and cold coming in through the window. The mother asked me how I was doing and I told her that I was fine. I told her, "I came to pay my respects," a term that I didn't know the meaning of but it was what my father always told me we were doing when we stood in front of that huge block of cement that held "The Unknown Soldier" in Virginia. It sounded stuffed and forced coming out of my mouth. The mother said thank you and smiled and seemed like she wasn't covered in plaster and in pain. Standing there in their living room, I was unable to detect any of the horror of what they had so recently been through. Only years later could I even attempt to imagine the loss.

Minutes later, I left sorry that I had gone in the first place.

Now years later, I know why the room felt the way it did. That's Death. Sometimes I can hear Death's clothing rustle as it walks next to me. Sometimes I feel its hand on my shoulder and everything looks alien.

I am a different species. I am falling apart into one solid piece. I feel secure in the futility of it all. I know there's really nothing of great importance in life.

Diner logic. When I finally got it through my head that no one cares and I'm on my own, things got clearer. I know people realize this but they blind themselves. I used to do that shit too. Sometimes I see myself slipping back into the lie. It's faith and hope that keeps them going. What fake fuel. I know what I know, and do I know it now. When you stare down the lie, you own yourself. When you own yourself, you win. Otherwise you're just another one of these assholes singing some stupid fucking song, getting all the words wrong as they wait for the bus to come.

Kiss of the tire iron. It's unbelievable to me how these celebrities never learn from history. They really think that no one will ever get tired of them. Suddenly, the people who adored them so much turn on them and move on to the next feast. They feel abandoned and betrayed. They thought they were immune to the process. They thought that somehow they were magically different and that people would be kissing their ass forever. The comedians survive better than the others do. The clowns last the longest but they get painted into their little corners. Imagine having to be funny all the time. To be that little version of yourself when the whistle blows. How weak. If you ever feel like standing for something, you'll have to be tough. They'll come after you. They'll try to break you. I won't be sticking around for them to cut me up. Fuck that. Idiots stick around too long. The smart ones do their little number, knowing that it's just their little number and get the hell out before they get run off. I'm not going to get too close to them. I know what they do when they do what they want. They treat you like a fucking piece of hotel furniture. Like a rental.

Put the Abyss to bed. I'll get a job in a basement tending to the furnace. Yeah, that's what I'll do. I'll be the guy who doesn't speak and never looks you in the face. I'll sit on an old milk crate with hissing embers to keep me company. I'll sleep in a room down the hall from the furnace. Every few days, the boss of the furnace will come down from above and ask me how the furnace is doing. I'll tell him it's fine in as few words as possible and hope it satisfies him. He'll walk away wondering about me. Wondering if I have a bad past, a prison record, war damage. He'll wonder why someone would actually take a job like the one I've got. He'll get on the elevator and walk into the sunlight and almost feel sorry for me. I'll feel like I am the luckiest guy in the world. I won't have to see anyone except on trips to the store. I won't have my dreams smashed. I won't have my bones broken anymore. I'll settle for the furnace. I'll not have the paranoia that keeps city dwellers wrapped so tightly. The flames will dance gently on my face. The room will be warm. I'll be able to get some reading done. I will outlast loneliness and not drive myself to the pathetic extremes I do now. Whenever I am pathetic and weak, it's because of loneliness and what I have done in my attempts to alleviate it. It's no good if you're not ready to settle for the lower levels of the mortal dilemma. Am I any different with my dreams of living in a small brick block carved out of earth below the sidewalk? I think about how their feet will walk right over me and they'll never know that I'm down there. I'll be so far below them I won't hear them, and that'll be ok by me. Maybe I can stay down there so long I'll start to forget. I'll forget to have nightmares. As it is now, I spit blood into the sink and think about smashing my brain to get it to quit. I wouldn't have to go out there and get my heart smashed apart anymore. That would be a relief. I don't think there's anything particularly great about being able to take that kind of punishment and survive. I mean, I don't think there's any kind of great lesson to be learned there. A hero for what? A hero for who? Always someone else. What a sellout. I always do it for them. To save face. To show them. I wasted so much of my time and ended up sick of the whole thing. I think about tending to the furnace for the rest of my life. That's how sick of it I am. What a monumental idea. To live underground for the rest of my life. To never see sunlight again. To never write another letter, to never make another phone call. It would be amazing to let it all go. Let go of ambition and jealousy. I wonder what else there would be to think about. I did my damn time out there with them. I'm finished. I think it was all a load. All the things that they said were important weren't. I think they were so mad that they got duped they feel the need to pass the lies and pain on to the next generation. You see all the ones that went for it. All the pain that they wanted for me... all the heartache that never seemed to stop breaking me. The monster it was turning me into. All those nights walking the streets looking at people and wanting to be part of it but knowing that I was never going to make it. I'm now ready to admit defeat to the masters of bullshit. I wasn't full of enough of it to toe the line. I'm ready to descend to the lower depths. I will tend to the furnace. Silence will be my epitaph.

Begging for another planet. It's good to pull out after so many years of sticking my neck out for imaginary people. I really thought they were there. It's a drag to see I have been taken to the cleaners by weaklings. I have stood in the way of evolution. The weak must not survive. I have learned to deflect and not let any of it stick to me. Can you imagine the idiocy of falling in love and getting all that time dragged out and starved to death? Trying to help someone in the name of who the hell knows who? How stupid. Too much ego. I retired from the whole torture session. It was interesting while I could still take the beatings. I lost my insecurities in the fray and no longer felt the need to walk amongst them. I think you should do what you want. If you want to be right, then I think you're the one who's right. If you don't want me that's ok, because I don't care. I don't care if you get my name wrong. It's ok by me because I know the truth. I know it doesn't matter. I know that when I'm empty no one has anything on me. You can't take what's not there. I'm safe in nothingness. I don't aspire to what you think has any worth. From you, I'm free at last.

Quickly, inject the dream. I pick up an unplugged phone and hear static. Then, I hear Joe's voice. He says he's in an energy field and the reception is bad. He says it's nothing but energy out there. No love or hate, no judgment. He says he's meeting a lot of people and none of them really know what's going on except that life is just the start. He says life on earth is a lightweight experience, a trial to see how you deal with energy, within the vanity of the human form. You think you know it all but you really know nothing. He goes on to say that suicide is such a joke. You might as well stick it out for as long as you can in your flesh because you eventually end up where he is anyway. You might as well get your kicks. He says that there's nothing to worry about and that people waste too much time worrying on earth. He says that people take life too seriously because they are convinced that's all there is and that's why they make war and kill each other and try to be the boss all the time. He says there's no cops where he is. He says it all made immediate sense to him as soon as he was out there. He says that I should hang in there and have a good time and be good to people even when they are bad to me. He says he doesn't envy the living. He says we carry too much fear and it's weighing us down, that we spend all our time trying to find the real meaning of life and it's right in front of us but we're too scared to see it. He tells me the rest was up to me. He fades out. I hang up.

Hang me in the closet by my collarbone. I don't trust any of them and I wish I could. I wish I could be close but they'll fuck you over every time. Make you look like a fool. You have to always play them like gangsters play their friends. Not like friends at all. Just someone who will eventually sell you out. If you're straight with them, then you get fucked over. The only way is to stay alone for as long as you can. You'll be better for it. It's hard but every time you let your shit down they'll use you and try to ruin you. I knew a girl years ago. She picked up on me. She tried to use me but I saw what she was doing because she was young and not very good at the play yet. I saw the whole thing unravel and always kept a few steps ahead of her. It's like I could read her mind. I had my fun and when she tried to go in for the kill, I just blew her off. I got a little on me, you always will with a scam artist, but I got out of it pretty clean. No problem there. I have my normal routine. Every time I get played by a woman, I make sure to do the same to one of them. I go out and find a girl who doesn't know anything and I mess her mind up. I figure they're all the same and if you get fucked over by one and you fuck over a different one for something she didn't do, then that's ok. You can play that poor me shit with some people but other people will crush you like an insect. You fuck with some people and they'll get revenge on others that you don't even know, years after the deed has been done. Like I'm going to stand around and let someone fuck me up. I don't think so. Men have been made to think they're supposed to be fucked over all the time. Too many people are afraid of what others think. Men are scared of everything. They'll do anything to get sex. Lie their asses off and compromise themselves. These men are losers and make the rest of the male population look bad. I'm just one of the species who won't tolerate being fucked over by a woman. There's not many men in the world with any backbone left. Real men got crowded out by weaklings who harnessed the power of finance and legal loopholes. Real power is determined by what you can do in the parking lot after the meeting is over. If the shit were real, I would be driving some lawyer's car right now. His scalp would be drying on the grill. Civilization's nearly over with. Your bullshit is falling to the ground. Your little morals are worthless and I'm getting my kicks telling the truth as you drown in your lies and cowardly weakness. You don't like the things I have to say? So? Survival species, motherfucker.

Done with rock and roll, ha ha ha. Where do you go after the storm is over? When all you know is pushing yourself until your body screams for you to stop yet you keep on? You go on. Senselessly on. What do you do with the velocity inside that still threatens to break you? When you have extended your threshold of pain to the point where it's all you know? When they say you can go home now and you don't know what home is. The hollowing descent of knowing that is hard to take.

They come up to you in the store and ask questions. They pick you off like an almost dead fish swimming close to the surface. You are something they can toy with and leave. All the years of work have caused an aura of fascination and now they come up and tear away small pieces of your skin. They hate you for reasons they don't know. Reasons they'll never take the time to think about. You feel that somehow what you did was wrong. That every time you gave it everything you had you were only setting yourself up to get slaughtered later on. An entire life dedicated unknowingly to your undoing. For them you were just entertainment. A clown. What a way to go out.

I went where the shadows are long and unmoving. I learned to become invisible. I see that there's nothing at the end of it all. You get your kicks and do your number before they kill you. The rest is just waiting it out.

Whitey flavored blues. I remember the nights. The nights spent so wisely. Each night spent like it was the last night on earth. So close to madness. So fucking close. Shrieking hours in hot, poorly lit rooms. Clawing the walls. Talking and screaming and laughing about a death trip. Mine. I cling to my memories of glorious desperation. It keeps me alive.

I dream of a woman who tastes like scar tissue. Fuel driven lies. Falling like rain. Flying by like bullets. Fixing and throwing up on my bathroom floor. I looked through your purse after you left the room. You had ripped me off. I took back my things and said nothing when you came back. You smiled and said it was nice to meet me. I'll bet after you found that I had taken back my stuff, it hadn't been so nice after all. As I was cleaning the puke off of the floor, I was thinking the same thing about you.

I'd like to break the armchair over your head. I like to destroy my sensitivity. I want to register pain. The more pain I can take, the stronger I become. Strength is all important. It will take me farther than your sensitivity will take you. You attack me intellectually but inside you fear me on a pure animal level. This makes you mad. You know I can see your fear. You know you broadcast it with every move you make. You know that I'm in control of the situation. You know I'm sparing you, yet at the same time I care nothing about your fractured sense of decency and your tiny morals.

You'll never know how much you hurt me. In an effort to save time, I now mutilate myself without her around to do it to me. I save on food and phone bills. I just go out and walk around until I see a beautiful woman. I follow her for a few blocks and get a good look at her. I do my best to smell her perfume. I then walk back to my room and lock the door. I imagine what it would be like to spend time with her. I think of the way we would meet. How she would see that I'm not like the others and feel safe in my company. She would trust me and want to be around me. I think of the things we would talk about while we were lying together in the dark. Then I think of the humiliation I will be put through in the weeks to come. The pathetic phone messages I will leave. The depression and fury I will endure until the wounds heal and only the scar tissue remains to remind me of my weakness and my great mistake. I can see her face and imagine her eyes burning into me. This is when I start stabbing myself with the large nail I carry on a string around my neck. The punctures vent dark blood and the pain is overwhelming. It's better than taking it over weeks. I get it all over with at once. I have been with some of the most beautiful women I have ever seen and they'll never know that they have been soiled by one of the great post-modernists of our time.

In the apartment building, there is always someone weeping alone and it sounds like summer rain hitting the window. There's no magic left in the world, my dear. You were the magic for me. In your eyes were all the secrets told only to me. In your embrace, I felt alive. Now you are gone and so is the magic and the great secrets of the universe. Now the streets are wide and cold. The voices are abrasive and the light is harsh. I feel so mortal as the weather turns cold. Hardly any trees on the streets here. When I was with you, we watched the leaves turn color and fall to the ground. Everything had significance and meaning. Now it all runs together and paranoia takes up most of my sleep time. I wait for something terrible to happen. I always felt safe with you. Now in all things, I see the bottom. I see through all things and I feel dangerous. I am frightened of what horrific acts of violence I could be capable of. In this urban environment, the animals are nonstop and I take their every move as a threat to my being. I have some instinctual need to survive but I no longer hold life as close as I did when you were here with me. You made all things vital. Now I am broken into pieces and I expect the scrap men to come in any time and sell me off piece by piece. One of my arms will end up on some guy who lost his in a factory accident. The parts of my brain that aren't damaged can be sold to people who were born with a defective model. But besides all of that, I miss your presence here with me. I account for time differently. Time seems to sit next to me like a quiet man on the subway. Time silently watches me in my room. I have no phone or radio and the only sounds I hear are traffic and people talking in the rooms on either side of me. Like I said before, there's no magic left in the world. I go out on the streets after work and I look. I can't find any. All I see is fear and fury, hunger and monster driven eyes. No magic. I do believe you might have taken it all with you when you went away.

I bear the scars of an old fool. Confront your fears early on. Reduce them to laughter and dust immediately. You must destroy them as soon as they rear their heads or they will own your life. It's the only way to survive the slaughterhouse that the gods of society have waiting for you. Find the extreme end of anything you're pursuing. Get there quickly and set up camp. Don't bother with the lighter side or the middle of any of it. It's only there to sell you something and waste your time. The place where most people aren't is where the real thing is. The more full-on the level of intensity, the less people you will see there. This is true without exception. Know that humans are inherently weak and not good for much. That's why you don't want to have too many around you for too long. If they see that you are strong they will be attracted to you. Beware, for this is also always true about humans without exception: they will eventually attack what is strong and see it as their enemy. In their fear they display their need to bring what is seemingly above and beyond them down to their level. You pay the price every time. Be secretive about your strength, protect your intelligence. See the end at the beginning before you make your first move. Take time to see all possible eventualities in any situation involving humans. Know that they don't value anything in their reach until it is gone. They envy, despise and fear what is beyond them. Why do you think the old stories tell of men who set out on great journeys to impress the gods? Because trying to impress people just isn't worth the time and effort.

I choke on shame and it rides through my dreams, screaming and laughing. I live far away from where I grew up because I can't walk those streets of failure ever again. I don't want to go down without swinging at all the demons, all the fuckers. I just want to be able to stand up straight for a little while before I get cut down.

A lifetime spent in the lion's mouth. I lived in the basement with the smells of alienation and dampness. I learned at an early age that they are mean. The FM radio played and I stayed up late looking at the walls that stood straight up under the ground. Smell of paint thinner and laundry. A few fish tanks of rats and snakes. School freak. Yeah, fuck you. Smash them, out earn them, out live them, bury them all. Spend time wanting to be like them. Maybe it's just getting the clothes right. I wanted them to like me and I wanted to be normal. I also knew there was no way, no fucking way.

The Evel Knievel of self humiliation. In my teens, I talked myself into calling a girl I used to play with when I was four years old. I had seen her come into the store I worked at. She was pretty. I got her number and it took several nights before I had the guts to call. Finally, I called and talked to her for a few minutes about maybe getting together sometime but it came out lame and awkward.

Crippled and damaged. Weak and twisted from too many nights in the basement listening to my mother walk upstairs. She told me to call her again the next night and I was happy. I called her the next night like she told me to. We were talking, but after a few minutes, I knew something was wrong. I heard laughing on the line and then she hung up. She had gotten one of her friends to come over and pretend to be her. The girl told a sister of a guy I knew and even she laughed at me. I remember the lump in my throat. Pain shakes your hand and says welcome to my world.

Diet of rocks. For some reason, the local boys up the street hated me. Seemed like it started overnight. One day I was walking home from school and they started fucking with me. Trying to get me into the street to fight. Tough, Irish Catholic boys with red hair and torn jerseys. People that I didn't know, didn't go to school with. These were aliens to my clenched jawed world. Why me? Why did these no-life shitheads have to treat me like that? I couldn't see it like that then. I knew I was going to have to take a new way home from school. Like I did the time after the man followed me all the way up to my door a few years before. Go to the basement and think of all the ways to kill them. Feel my guts start to attack each other when I would get to the block where they always seemed to be lounging outside their parent's places. It was like they had no other purpose in the world except to wait for the one stick man to walk by them with his eyes glued to the ground. I hated the world before I hit puberty.

You can find me in the frozen mood section. Intelligence is life insurance. Strength is currency in the bank. Even in this age where you can go out and get shot in the stomach and die screaming in front of a convenience store, you need all the strength you can get. More power now. I stalk the room well past midnight, unable to sleep. My thoughts driving me to move, to stop questioning things logically and become the definition of the word action. Without strength what do you know, what chance do you have out there? People have separated themselves from their survival instincts in the name of civilization. Yeah, well that bullshit shows its colors as soon as the going gets rough.

Around the world on a Greyhound bus. Sometimes I wish I could be like Teflon. I always admired that stuff. Water beads up on it and slides off, nothing sticks. You gotta have a little of that to be able to deal with what's out there. But... Teflon takes a shot and shows the damage. It cannot heal itself. That is our strength; we can heal. We can make ourselves stronger. You can be a bright light in a sea of shit, doesn't matter how big the light is as long as it shines. Get a hold of some of that and don't blow your brains out no matter how good an idea it sounds like at the time. Like when you wake up around three in the morning panicking from an attack from some unseen horror and you want to get out so bad.

Sweat in January. You know the time where you say to yourself that you've never felt this bad before? But you say that every time. The pain is real. How do you gauge your desperation? What do you do in those situations where you're held captive and slave to your crashing emotions? Times where you make a pathetic fool out of yourself. I once knew a woman. She left me and told me to leave her alone. The things I said, and the letters that I wrote to her, I am ashamed of to this day. I was desperate and my brain was running wild. I remember sitting in my room for days afterwards, looking at the floor and thinking that this is what it's like when someone dies. I had never felt that bad before, I've felt worse since. So have you. How do you control yourself when it all hurts so much? Even if you could make someone understand you, so what? You're on your own, so on your own. How do you deal with winds that make your bones moan and nights that make you sweat and panic? The answer never seems to come. You just keep breathing until it fades. When someone says they have the answer, that means they don't have shit.

You get beat in and you get beat out. The bad thing about the entertainment business is that all the little parasites who make a living off you have something to do with the way people perceive you. It's too bad that the pen is often mightier than someone who could break your fucking neck with his hands. Unless you do this for a living, you will never know how much work goes into all of it. You know nothing of the sacrifice and single-minded focus needed to put it together and get it out there. There's always someone who will take several months of your life and trivialize it in a few paragraphs. Nothing you can do but get over it or not pay attention. I have learned to do both. I don't have another lifetime to dick around with the tiny masters of today. I just go, stupidly on. I pull back every once in awhile to look around and see who I'm in front of, who I'm giving everything I've got to. I look at the mail at my feet and read how I've sold out by doing this or by playing there. Some twenty one year old boy telling me how I sold out. I just take it, what else am I going to do, tell the guy the truth? Spend the better part of half an hour trying to assure him that I'm an alright guy and that my intent is only aimed at good? Why should I? I used to. What you thought of me really used to matter. But after catching several projectiles in the face, reading lies about myself in magazines, spending so many years working at all this shit, I have forgotten how to do things for myself—I no longer care what you think of me. You will eventually forget and move on to something else anyway. It is very possible that after all the years of exhaustion and ceaseless servitude, I could end up on the street living in a cardboard box. I could end up some pathetic leech looking for a break, willing to do anything to get noticed. It may well be that I could turn out to be one of those people you see at a club one night and say, "Oh my god it's that fuckin' guy! What was his name?" That could happen—if I blindly believed in the gratitude and warmth of a bunch of fucking strangers. But I don't. In fact, I count on the worst. I'm gearing up for the revenge part of my life. It's going to be so good. After I get beat out the other end of this, I'll still be walking straight because you will never be strong enough to break me. I will be sane and in great health. I will have money in the bank and wisely invested. This will be the best revenge I can imagine. Understand this—I never believed anything you told me. When you hurt me, it never hurt as much as the pain I brought upon myself. I never did any of this shit for money. You could stack dollars miles high and it wouldn't be enough for what I gave of myself. The only thing you could repay me with is time, and since you don't have any that you can add to my life expectancy, don't ever tell me we're even, or that I owe you. I owe you nothing. Not even the truth.

12 on the 31st. It was Halloween night and there was a guy walking home from work like he did five nights a week at pretty much the same time. His walk was interrupted when an egg hit him. He heard laughter and looked around. Twelve youths were looking at him and pointing. He looked down and saw a bottle, picked it up and threw it at the boys. Immediately they surrounded him so he couldn't get away. One ran off and returned a moment later with a handgun. The boy shot the man in the neck and killed him. The man on the news went from this right into a great story about an eleven year old girl that was sexually molested on the stairs of her school by other students. Next up, sports. In the room I'm in, the heater is on and I can't shut it off. I have the air conditioner on to try to balance it out. The room stinks of old heater smell and old A/C fluid. It's past five in the morning and I can't sleep. I'm not complaining. I feel lucky. As shitty as this place is, at least I'm alone and not out there with you. Great close-up of some blood and a bullet casing right after the commercial break.

The minimum, always. In the dream, I was in the hospital with running sores on my legs. There were others in beds along the wall. All of a sudden, one of them would break into a long painful howl that would trigger all of them to go off in the same manner. I passed out. I woke again and heard them chanting, "We have no use," over and over. A woman came to my bedside and stared at me. She touched my cheek with her hand. I could feel something in my throat. I opened my mouth and a large insect came out, crawled off the side of the bed and disappeared. She had no reaction to this. I stared into her eyes. She turned into a snake, a flower, a pack of lies. Today I wore long pants to cover the scars on my legs from where my father cut strips of my flesh away to feed himself. He beats me regularly when I let him into the living room. He says he needs to, it keeps him young. He says that he had me so he could feed off me. It makes sense so I let him do it. I guess I could do the same with my offspring. Isn't that why you have children in the first place?

Full time stranger. I am a lot like you were, my dead friend. I **J**ust wanted them to stay. I would do anything to make them stay with m**E**. I would tell them anything. I lowered myself to disgusting depths. I was pathetic. I knew how it would be when they le**F**t. So lonely. You know how it is when you spend time with someone and after they're gone, you sit there looking around the room trying to **F**igure out how it's different. The same room that you were laughing in now feels like a suffocating wound of so**R**row and depression. Time slows down. The loneliness is unbearable. You go over the things you talked about and say some of th**E** things out loud and try to laugh at the jokes but it's no use. **Y**ou're alone in your room and the light in the ceiling feels like it's looking at you, stalking you. Believe it or not, there are people who have no idea of what this kind of emptiness is like. They never go through it. You might think that is impossible but I know this for fact. Some people are never alone. Not like you an**D** me. Never like us. Eternally **A**lone. Alone even in company. You go outside to try and get over it. You go to a crowded place. You look in the windows of bars as you walk. You try to imagine yourself sitting on a stool talking to someone and not feeling lonely but the more you try, the more dislocated you feel. I know what it's like to be **H**ated. I know what it's like to be hunted. I know the scream that sits underneath the skin but never breaks through. It drives you **M**ad. I know the pain of everything you say coming out wrong. I know what it's like to feel like a monst**ER**. When you told all the relatives you were sorry that you killed members of their families, I believed you. I could see it in your eyes. I believed it when you said you only wanted them to stay because you were lonely. I believe that every day you sat in prison you missed them still. You only wanted them to stay. You only wanted someone to be there. On the news they showed photos of you sitting on your bunk in the Army years before you killed those men. Even then, I could see the loneliness and confusion in your eyes. I bet you were thanking them as they beat your skull in. I bet you were telling them you only wanted them to stay and that you were sorry, so very sorry.

My skin tastes like the sidewalk. I tried for years to understand you and all I did was destroy myself. Now I'm going to turn it around. I will not hide my contempt or hatred any longer. All the time I spent in suffocating humiliation. You have not seen cruelty like mine. I come from the desert of starvation. The lean years made me tough and strong. All the time you thought you were killing me, you were just making me stronger. I am now solid scar tissue. Fuck your values. Fuck your morality. You are a planet of snakes. Different names, different faces. All the same beast. You're so cunning. The other day I watched you draw pity out of someone I paid to destroy you. It was horrible to watch how you were able to convince him to show you mercy. In my world there is no mercy for you and your kind. Today I listened to another one of you talk endlessly and had to breathe in the noxious fumes as the babble raged on. I made up my mind at that point I was through with you. I was through with the torture. I feel better already. I will do to you what you taught me. I will pass my fingers over my scars and read them like Braille and they will tell me what to do. I will act accordingly. My mistake was thinking I was human and that I could take part in the rituals. My other mistake was thinking that taking the same punishment over and over was teaching me something. I think you were the ones who made up the idea that pain builds character. It keeps us coming back to get destroyed over and over. Pretty soon we think that is just the way it is and learn to live with the pain. Not all of us. Not me. Not anymore. I am stupid, so the few things that seep through only stick because they were beaten into me. Now you're fucking with an institutionalized animal. See my face? It's part you, part what you made me. I have disappeared into you. You are the Solipsist, I am nothing but an extension of you.

I want to fill my head with concentrated nothing. That way I could withstand having to listen to you for the rest of my life. I don't like the way my voice sounds. I don't like the shit that comes out of my mouth. Sometimes I talk, I can't even believe it's me. I hate the need for me to talk. Afterwards, I feel stupid. I feel I should keep my mouth shut. I should lock myself away so I won't talk to anyone. I look at them when I talk. They nod their heads, smile, laugh. They are humoring me. They would rather I just shut the fuck up. I can tell by looking at 'em. I don't mix well with people. I talk to keep them at a distance. I talk to fool myself into believing I am something I am not. I talk, I mask my confusion with conviction. I need to bolster my sore, fragile ego. I fool no one.

From now on all you get is the rough back hand, the fist full of claws, bushels of thorned branches, the purest bile and all the wrath I can muster. It will come from the heart and soul so don't think that I've sold you out. It's just going to hurt the both of us that much more. It took years of screwing up every almost-friendship I ever had to figure out how to maintain one. You can't tell your friends the truth about yourself at all. Avoid any below the surface level, personal, truthful fact or admission when you're dealing with anyone you want to keep as a friend. Always lie to them for your sake and theirs. Never give them the slightest glimpse of the sick, horrifying darkness that rages inside you. The depression that makes you blind with homicidal fury. The eternal bleak nights when all you want to do is die. Otherwise you will lose them. You will alienate them and they, in turn, will judge you. No matter what they tell you they will hold the differences between you, against you. And since no one believes it when you tell them that everything is fine every time they ask, I tell them about problems I don't really have, ones that any idiot could reason their way out of. They need to hear some problem so they can help you with it. It gives them a sense of power when they can help you "solve" your dilemma. They will always think they did it for you. It will give their ego a boost because it will make them feel like they have some great knowledge. They will take away a feeling of worldly power they would never lower themselves to ever holding over you. In their mind, the whole process draws the two of you closer because they feel they provided you with a perspective and an insight you lacked. They will always talk highly of you when you're not around because they have helped you and they know that you are the grateful student of their wisdom. They will always be happy to help you later on because the need to solve the problems of others is something that the ego never gets enough of. So even when the advice they give you is pedestrian and as helpful as an empty wallet, act like it's a small revelation. You will have a friend for life. I don't want to be alone all the time. I want to have friends. So I never tell them the truth. I am good at this, therefore I have many friendships that have lasted a long time. As well, you never know if any one of your "friends" are doing the same thing to you, so always be helpful when a friend comes calling. Live a clean enigmatic life. Leave a good looking corpse. Always be unknown.

The clothes you wear tell the rest of the world something about you, don't they, sure they do. Wearing a bow tie says a few things; one of them is, "I don't have sex so I'm wearing this tie instead." Another is "I am a pathetic clown with no self-esteem so to take away your opportunity to ridicule me, I will do it to myself first. For instance, feature my tie." Something happened and all the world's population was miraculously stripped of violence, hatred and anger. All was peaceful and people smiled and said "peace" to each other but it didn't mean much because everything was already peaceful, so completely peaceful. It was like if someone came up to you, held their hands out in front of them and said, "air." Yes, it's there but the gesture is one of the emptier ones I've heard. Around this time a few people, well a lot of them actually, came to my place and asked me to come out and talk to them. I was wary because only a short time earlier they told me there was no room for me in their city on account of all my violence, hatred and anger. The miraculous peace event apparently had no effect on me, so I was politely asked to leave the city limits. I moved to the sticks and hung out with the trees and the animals. It was not half bad. Better than these people running up and hugging me all the time, asking if I wanted to try some sunflower seed bread or if I wanted to get high. So anyway, these people came knocking one morning and asked if I could teach them to hate again. I told them that it could be done but it was going to cost them. I was, of course, thinking of the possible spin-offs, video rights, pay-per-view and other anger related products. So many marches and demonstrations trying to get peace in the world, all those disgusting rock concerts and overblown pseudo-intellectuals like Bob Geldof acting like they were more than mere money seeking slobs with their noses pressed intently into the panties of empty headed morons like the one he eventually married. The road to peace was a long journey littered with concert t-shirts, Ben and Jerry's "Rainforest Crunch" ice cream containers and stupid songs like "We Are the World" and "I Don't Like Mondays." I asked these laid back intruders why they wanted hatred back in their lives. "We are fucking bored and we want to fuck shit up but dammit, we have forgotten how." Of course this information was rendered in a peaceful manner as they sat on the ground in front of me fingering their beads. In a matter of minutes, I had them signed to a lifetime contract giving me 15% of whatever their action was. Lesson one started immediately. "All the sluts line up against this wall. Let's go." No one moved, they just stared at me blankly. "Don't know who that is? I'll make it easy for you, if you don't have a dick in your pants, then line the fuck up against the wall." The women stood up with confused looks on their faces. "What did you call us?" one of them asked. "I'm sorry, you lesbian." I replied. "I meant to say, 'would all you penis envying castrators please line the fuck up against the wall.'" The women's faces broke out in angry scowls and then into broad smiles. "Thank you for restoring our anger, you typically insecure component of the cowardly, soon-to-be-toppled white male power structure!" one them said. "No problem, flat ass." I replied, making sure to address her chest. One of the guys spoke up, "What about us?" I turned to the men who had all gathered together. "You guys walk ten paces over there and start throwing rocks at each other's heads." "When do we stop?" "When all of you feel the overwhelming urge to run for office," I replied. The women watched the men for awhile and told them what a bunch of boring and violent assholes they were and the men told them that they should be home making babies and pot roast and shutting the fuck up. Away they walked, bickering, back to the city. One of the men turned back and said, "Thanks, fuckhead." Within days all was well with the world.

A 400 year old Aztec with tears in his eyes suddenly materializes in front of you and asks you why his temple has been destroyed, why the remains are covered with vines and tourists are peeling away layers of the temple's soul with their cameras? His confusion and amazement is almost child like in its innocence. For some reason, he thinks you can help him. You shrug your shoulders and offer him a beer. He screams and turns to dust. I remember reading an account of a convict who was hanged for murder. He stayed alive awhile because he had strong neck muscles and was not dropped far enough to snap his spine. I used to think of him, swinging alone with the bag over his head while people watched from the other side of the cloth. I remember a guy telling me that before this one man was hanged he was asked if he had any last words and he said, "Death is as light as a feather." I can see my breath. Strange for Miami but it happens out here near the sinkholes. The guy shoved me into the back of the car so hard that I lost my balance and hit my forehead on the roof. I remember hearing laughter, cursing and someone sitting down next to me. The smell of alcohol filled breath. Colombians. I hope it's over quick. They shoved my brother's wife's arm down the sink and turned on the disposal. My brother was tied to a chair and made to watch. They told me. Short drive down a dirt road to a tree on the side of what looks like a driveway. Three men and me. I am pulled out and told to sit on the ground. The headlights shine through the dust that the men are raising. I feel tired even though my adrenaline is pushing my heart into my throat. A boot toe in my ribs. Time to get up. Death will not be light as a feather. I did not steal their cocaine. I have covered for my brother before. I think of his wife going into shock and bleeding to death in the hallway outside their apartment. She never knew. Pulled to my feet by my hair. Arms around my waist. Thick wire with a metal clamp to cinch the loop. Two men push my head through and push down on my shoulders until the wire bites into my flesh. The last thing I remember seeing is my brother being pulled out of the trunk and forced to watch. I hear him screaming, "I'm sorry Jerry I'm sorry. Oh god please don't he's my brother." I die at a little past three in the morning in the winter of 1971.

Don't worry. It will never be you. You'll never get a scratch and no one will remember your gutless music. Don't get mad. You don't want to pay the price for being real. It's more than your stooped back stoned bony ass could ever take. Now step the fuck aside and let a real man destroy himself in front of the masses. No. You sweep it up. You scrub the spot and make the stain come out if you can't deal with the memory of yourself. Don't call me. Don't contact me. Don't try to find me. Don't attempt to lie and make yourself think I will someday return to you to help you save yourself from your mind-destroying existence. Make friends with the night. Stop denying despair. It is time for you to throw yourself to the plague of the room. Kiss the walls and familiarize yourself with them. Stop crying. No one's watching now. Tears don't matter anymore, they don't do anything but fall from your face silently. Don't you get it? Finally, it's here. Your real life is staring you right in the face. This is how it is. Yeah. Smell the tobacco and alcohol. The stale smell of sweat and unpaid rent. Here it is. No more road. No more favors. No more not having to be. Now you gotta be real all the time or someone will throw your ass out into the street. Better for you to shield yourself from the fact that few will remember your dubious glory days. Yeah, they know you. They recognize you standing in line for food stamps with all the other legends and they feel two things: pity for you, and stupid—for ever having been into your shit in the first place. What moved you to ever think that any of these people were your friends? You never liked them. You only liked the power you held over them. You were addicted to it. Don't fuck a fan. Don't fuck the help. Don't fuck someone wearing a t-shirt with a picture of you on it. You called them stupid sluts after they left. What did you think you were? What does your life make you? Take the facts of your life and look at them. What do you got? Yeah, that's right. No. You pick it up. You go get it. Stop pounding on my door. Stop embarrassing yourself. Finally, do something besides being pathetic.

I ignore you because if I acknowledge your existence then I will have to acknowledge myself as existing and then there's the risk of remembering a fragment of what I have been working so hard to forget—myself. In moments of silence and isolation, I can make myself believe that life is merely passing through me uninterested like wind through an abandoned town. The only thing I fear now is clear and total recognition of my own distinct wretchedness. What is sickening is that I am fascinated by it like it was someone else's. I research my life like I was doing a book on a person long dead. I walk the old streets and take notes of where and when. I force myself to re-live the most humiliating and brutalizing events of my life like they were right now—but always in the third person. I look at an apartment building and write down that at one time "he" lived there. I make note of all the things that were done to him there. All the things that he did to himself; all the things that he thought in his inexhaustible moments of weakness. When things are good, I live as a stranger to myself and I can breathe with an ease born of ignorance and denial. When in those terrible moments of self-recognition of my pathetic self-destructive fury, I want unexistence. I want to find a place where I can live in darkness and silence forever. I think of living on the moon. Either this, or abuse and harm randomly. Either null and void knock out time or eternities spent convulsing ceaselessly at the horror of myself. The disgust of seeing myself in their faces. Even worse to feel their touch. These words will be lost in the storm's howl. They reside in small rooms, ground into old carpet. They are choked and uncalled for. They will remain unclaimed until time cannot be bothered to draw another breath. Here I am. Down I go. Here are the shadows. Here is my disappearance into the anti-mind. My final flight. I see myself and now I know that everything will be the way I want it to be.

Note found next to the body: "Every day I don't humiliate myself, I feel stronger somehow. Staying away from that which would destroy me is to possess a small victory. It seems that the things I want are those that come with the danger of hurting me in ways I cannot cope with. The pain of loneliness is great, but nothing compared to the wretchedness of humiliation and abandonment.

I hate myself for my cowardice but at the same time I compliment myself for not walking willingly into the slaughterhouse thinly disguised as shelter. I'd rather walk through a moonless night on frozen wasteland crust than feel the burn that your agonizingly graceful apathy brings. You can blow me off your shoulder like a speck of ash. I'll float silently and invisibly to the ground, unnoticed. So in order to not have to endure this, I move quickly and wordlessly through urban landscapes. Every day I feel a sense of accomplishment. When I think of you, all I see is a banded spitting cobra with unmoving, unreadable black eyes. Mouth slightly open. Always ready to attack. And now the part that I hate to admit. I am frail and you are all I think about. I am powerless to stop. I have always loved you. Long after you forgot my name. Long after the leaves left the trees and fell through frozen air. I was never strong enough to stop the pain from crippling me. This is my last effort to get your respect and maybe a drop of your affection, full of pity as it may be." I didn't feel the fangs when she bit into my flesh. My eyes were full of wonder, staggered by her beauty and entranced by her gaze. I was lost in my own world of pain. I learned that there would always be pain when I was with her and pain when I was without her. Each time my eyes were opened to the face of the snake, they were blinded by her smile. My ravaged senses were merely numbed by her embrace, never healed. I learned this over and over as the years passed and I ran low on blood. She will always make you take the pain. I must be strong because I need her.

She is all that is toxic and all that burns the skin. Her saliva is poison. Her secretion is cancerous. She drains the soul and never stops taking. She lifts her hand and crops die. When she stands in anger, locusts darken the sky, forests burn to the ground and nothing ever grows again, the seas grow rancid and calm as all life underwater ends. We keep coming back. We keep getting scarred and our flesh gets burned.

She lives in all of them. Different faces, same snake. I had to cut up a few to find out. You always have to cut a few to find out. Another head sprouts from the stump. This is continuous. If she is destroyed she re-creates herself instantaneously and resumes without hesitation.

You will never kill her. To kill her you have to kill all of them and you never will. You will be stopped by those who don't see the evil they are. They will kill you like an animal in the street. The same people who will be paying with their own lives as they are slowly drained of their blood and choked to death by the snake that will not die, that will not stop inflicting pain.

I begged her to be kind, to stop biting and spitting her venom into me. She did not take heed of my plea and kept killing me. I ran away as she laughed. She knew I would be back some day, locked eye to eye with a different version of her, powerless.

She knows her beauty is overpowering and eternal. She lives only to destroy and paralyze. She demolishes and ruins. She knows no other way. Read the books and see the scars on your own flesh. Look at all the time you have wasted as you selflessly tried to give her everything only to have her lie to you and attempt to destroy you while she smiles and makes you beg.

The truth is a black spitting cobra. The streets are full of spitting cobras. When a body dies, they jump into another. The moon reflects off their backs and they move silently. Their beauty is more powerful than a million geniuses.

I stood with my hands out while she bit and spat. I watched her kill me. Her eyes did not close; her expression did not change. The only sound that came from her was a slow, controlled exhalation of air.

You think that the old history books were full of lies? What about the ones that will come out in one hundred years? If they come out at all. I was standing in line at the grocery store. A man ahead of me had full blown AIDS. *Check our new vocabulary. My parents never spoke in terms like these. They didn't speak the new language of fear. They will never know the lifetime of paranoia that awaits us. We are the pioneers of the wilderness created by their mistakes and morality. We will pay like they never had to. They never saw it coming.* He was speaking to his friend loudly about me like I wasn't there. I asked him how much time he thought he had left. The checkout man dropped a can of soup. The man looked at me slightly startled and said, "I don't know. I don't really think about it." I said, "I don't believe you. I think you think about it all the time. I think it keeps you up at night. I think that your sleep is nothing but your body's exhaustion rising to a level that overcomes your fear. I think your nights are full of blank time staring into the darkness wondering about when you are going to die. The meditations on your death override the pain your body is in. You have learned the painful truth about your friends. They cannot hide their fear and sadness. It hurts you to see them feel so badly for you because you know their feelings are real but at the same time they are thinking about themselves and wondering if they could end up the same way. You think of your parents and how much you miss them even though they're not dead. Am I right?" He and his friend just stared at me. The check out guy handed the man his change and the two of them mutely walked away. The man's friend carried the bag of food. There's no rules anymore. Things don't last when they don't work. Morals don't work so they don't last either. Anything you need to protect with a gun isn't bound to last. So here we are walking through the neon strip mall wasteland. It is a wasteland, you know. It's wasted and lost like a lot of things, like a lot of people. We are so cold and isolated under the stars. We are digital renderings of ourselves.

Southern Californian. Steeped in sunlight and shallow top soil. Unsure terra firma. Flakey job references. Police record, just a little one. Fuckin' around with the guys, you know. Idiot. Unable to live outside of the pollution roof and bullet-ridden terrain. Thinking about making that move to Las Vegas. No redeeming qualities. Army-Navy, nowhere else to go, why not? Didn't do it for the education. Did it because I got kicked out of the house and my drums got ripped off. You always know the true colors when they split their bad metal band for the military. They were future cops all along but didn't know it yet. The room has no chairs. I sit on the floor. I like to be below the windows as much as possible to avoid being seen; it cuts down the possibility of getting caught in the path of a stray bullet, a natural cause of death in my area. I only communicate with myself; that's why I write so much. *I weakly try to impress with my poor arsenal of verbiage and meager writing skills.* It passes time. When I was young, I always stayed on my own. I figured out at an early age that it was better to be able to stand alone. *I hope you always had a trace of fear when I fucked you.* In solitude there was pure strength. Thoughts were more clear and all senses were sharper when I had a minimum of human contact. *Truth is, I wanted to be like you in every way. (I even bought the same clothes, hoping some of it would rub off on me. Didn't work.) But I was never fast enough, smart enough or coordinated enough so I made being a spastic screeching monkey child my main task. It's easier to fail.* Several years later, I am still the same. I hardly notice the time. Decades of being a loner have left me with next to no social skills to use in situations where dealing with people is mandatory. I act. I gesture. I use as few words as possible. Their world holds nothing for me. I have been all over the world and met many people. I left it. *Actually, I couldn't handle it so I had to leave before I was discovered and torn apart. A career in the entertainment industry seemed like a logical choice.* There's some things that I know. I have sat so still in this room for such long periods of time that all I was doing was existing. I never got it together. *I live in an infantile world of my own creation where I am the oppressed and sensitive man of steel.* This is real life, straight time. Just me and me into infinity. Isolation Man blasting off to where all trails end. Everywhere is nowhere and nowhere is everywhere, right here. *Used to living in fear of supplies running out.* Feeling fine with nothing. Feeling fine at the end of the line. Running my fingers over the scars. Slowly extinguishing the candle image memories, one by one. I wait for nothing, no one. I don't have dreams of romance, no visions of beauty. *I dream of romance all the time but cannot take the humiliation that goes with having to be real with someone else.* Where I am there is no love or hate.

One of those self-satisfied, smirking, "I'm always going to be fine even if you won't" kind of guys that you want to belt in the mouth immediately. No that's not me. It's just my image! 3 a.m. Hot apartment, unmoving air, desk lamp lighting the room. Like sitting in an egg. My cubicle, my cell, my big mistake.

I used to sit in a chair and spin for hours. Down to my underwear, sweating. Going nowhere all the time and sick of being reminded of it.

I would get off work and walk back to my apartment and take my seat at the bow of the USS Nowhere. Vacant. Couldn't get a grip on my frustration. I was grinding myself into the dirt and sure I had enough money to live on but it wasn't enough. I sat at my desk. I didn't write. I didn't talk. I just bummed out. Night after night.

That was my insanity. That was living in a cancerous swamp. Endless quicksand dream. The day was the night and the night was the day. It all melted and ran together and I tried to keep my head above it.

My job: A dough folding brainwash machine. I walk in the door, the machine pulls at me, stirs me into the batter, stamps me into shape and spits me out. I used to come out of the door feeling like I had been kidnapped by a gang of retards and teased until I screamed.

Why am I sitting here thinking of all this? I saw a person from this time period the other day. That shit tripped me out. I'm sitting behind the counter of the hotel I work at, looking through the list of wake up calls I have for the morning. I hear this voice say, "Hello stranger." I look up and there she is staring at me. I was so surprised I couldn't say much besides the regular hello how are you type thing. She talked to me, I don't remember much of what she said, I was tripping out on her face too much. My brain started to climb all over the place, remembering the hot nights and hot days, white hot sheets wet with sweat, slept in alone. Walking to work, eating out of cans, standing in front of the refrigerator drinking out of cold bottles of water to try and cool down the hate, cool down the depression, stop the walls from closing in, stop the roaches from crawling on my face. She says, "I heard you were working here. What have you been up to? I haven't seen you in a couple of years." I tried to think of what I had done and I said a few things that I didn't mean and don't remember and I'm looking at her eyes and I'm looking at her hair and I'm looking at her mouth and I'm remembering the first time I ever met her and that must have been four, five, six, seven years ago. And some words are falling out of my mouth in disarray but my brain is screaming very clearly: *Why did you come here? Do you remember the things I said to you? Do you remember the things we did? Do you remem-*

ber? Do you remember the times you used to come by my job and talk to me and drive me out of my mind? Do you remember how it went back and forth and through and up and down and then took off and went nowhere? Crummy, used, stupid, weak, small and embarrassed are a few of the things I remember feeling.

And she says, "I've been working in LA." And I say, "That must be great," or something. I mean, I don't know what to say to her, just standing there.

She said that she had to go because she had someone waiting for her in a car out in front. She leaned over the counter, kissed me and left. My brain! Scream! Bend! Hot room! Empty room! Hot air! Vacant starvation life, in and out of the day to day. Heart beating like a clock and I know you can't stop time but you can let it heal lonely wounds and then a word comes from someone's mouth and lays you open again and the words: weak stupid, used, lonely, small, pathetic, down and out and going nowhere assault you and kick you around with one hand tied behind their backs. Oh! Dumb brain. If my brain had any brains it would forget everything. If my brain had a heart, it wouldn't do this to me and I know that no one can do it to me better than I can but help like this is help I don't need. It's the kind of help that leaves you helpless and then leaves you every way but alone. Oh! My brain is a twenty-four hour fast food library video laundromat. I close my eyes, in goes a quarter—swimming pool nipple push cold water hand grab cold blooded hand slap bikini cloth tight mind drool—make memo to punish cock later in the vacancy of own room.

I went back to the list of wake up calls. I stared at the front door of the hotel. I see that door five nights a week. Now it will always be the last door I saw her walk out of. Night after night, I looked at that door. I retraced her footsteps to the counter. I looked at the spot where her elbows had been. Let it go. Let it die.

The frozen men of the Bowery. They walked through cold to eat. They waited in line to sleep. They watched the street for signs. They waited for nothing and it came and stayed and never left. The air was freezing this morning. Sky was clear over the beaten up buildings on the Bowery. I watched the men come out of the shelter. A lot of soldier gear worn. Makes sense for them. It has been a low level, subtle war for decades out here. They know they're on the front lines even if millions don't see it even though they walk through it every day. A man sleeps on a piece of cardboard. He's covered with blankets in the middle of it all. The sky is piercing blue. I read the old painted advertisements on the walls of the buildings. You can see the assured optimism in the styling of the letters. Now it would be a con that no one would believe. I sometimes refuse to acknowledge this age. I listen to music several decades old. I read writers long dead. I want to know old facts and hear old stories. I am repulsed by several aspects of modern culture. It is sad and vacant. An old burlesque dancer trying to keep up appearances utilizing the latest technology. No memory of what got her there in the first place. I think in the future there will be a lot of things happening that I will absolutely not be showing up for. I will learn to more efficiently dodge the upload of useless information and media overload. It will be the only way to stay clean. I am drawn to this neighborhood. The janitors walking to work. Their worn clothes and tough hands. The beaten down men staring at the ground. I saw a malt liquor can suspended in a frozen puddle in the gutter. The men on the Bowery have wet eyes and time. Beyond humiliation, ambition or concern. Always makes me wonder if there's a calm that hits you when you realize you can sink no further. When you hit the bottom and the ground is unquestionably underneath your feet. I know they know something I don't. They have been standing in the end zone for years. The men pushed together as they await the end. They move slowly like livestock about to be herded into the train. They talk amongst themselves. Hair matted in the position in which they slept. A question I asked myself as I walked back to the room: When you recycle or throw trash into trash cans, not contributing to the litter and waste on the ground, are you making the immediate area around you a better place or are you merely polishing the gears of the machine that imprisons you every day? The garbage truck swallowed several bags of trash outside of the men's shelter and they exploded, shooting rotting food all over the street. The garbage men cheered and the pigeons went wild. The men in front of the shelter watched in silence.

I am strapped to a metal slab. A tube is in my arm draining my blood. There is a tube going into my other arm. I see that it's a slow drip IV bottle. The label says that the bottle contains applause. I am being filled with applause. I can feel the hands clapping in my veins. My heart is pounding with appreciation. The last things I remember were my heart exploding and the roar of a standing ovation filling my ears. I have figured out the way I want to die. I think of different ways all the time. I have put a lot of thought into this. I do not want to go out from old age. I want to go out with a little more drama than just a fade out. I don't want people to be able to walk by me and pat me like a fucking dog. I want my death to be the stuff of legend. Not one where I have to take out other people on my way down, how weak. I want it to be more than suicide. Suicide is intense but not the way I want to be remembered. It's not radical enough. Not controlled enough. You probably want me to get to the point and tell you the way I want to die. Ok, here it is. I want to freeze to death. I want to walk through a desolate ghetto of ice, snow and grey sky. I will be well dressed because I don't want to go that quickly. I want to last at least twelve hours. I want a good fight. I want to walk away from people and never see another one. I want to walk away and hear no human sounds, no machines. I want to experience nothing but nature's cruel precision. After several hours I will begin to hallucinate. I will think I am the only human on earth. Maybe I will think I am walking on the moon. Maybe I will make it through the night and maybe I won't. As the cold starts to take me away, I will be aware that I am living for real for the first time. No people, no pressure, no one to impress or lie to. There will just be me and my mortality. It will all go with me. I like this because I have always hated weakness. I think it would be great to confront death and walk to it, but make it work to get me. Nothing sudden like a gunshot. I want to go down fighting. Not for any cause, not for the cameras, just for the sheer glory of going into a battle I know I am going to lose and going in anyway.

I have always been fascinated with the effects of cold ever since I read Jack London's, *To Build a Fire.* I would walk to school in the winter wearing a thin warm up jacket that was a few sizes too small just to feel the numbing effects of cold. My friends thought I was crazy. The cold taught me things I was not learning in school. The cold hurt and made time drag as I walked to the school bus stop. Other students would be standing there bundled up and I would stand next to them in my blue jacket with white stripes going down the arms. Seeing them warm and layered in clothes their mothers put on them made me feel tougher than them. I was a poor student so I went through some strange self-imposed rites of passage to build up some confidence.

During the winter of my senior year in high school there was a snow storm that closed down the area schools. I went to visit my girlfriend who lived far away from me in the suburbs. I figured out the bus route and went. I got off a long way from her place and walked the rest of the way in. This was great stuff for me. A small adventure. When I finally arrived at her place, my face was so cold I could barely talk. She thought I was strange.

A couple of years later I was working at an ice cream store. We had a big walk in freezer, the kind that employees are ordered into and executed in by robbers. This is where we would store the week's worth of ice cream. At night we would bring ice cream to the freezers upstairs so it could warm up enough for us to scoop it the next day. There was a down jacket next to the door of the freezer in case you had to stand in there a long time when ice cream barrels were coming in off of the truck. I always fantasized about being locked inside the walk in freezer. A few times I had my friends close the door on me and then open it a minute later. In that moment in the dark with the frozen air blasting it occurred to me that I could die in there. This made the walk-in freezer a special place. You could die in there, that was an intense thought for me then.

Ever since then, I have been intrigued by intense climate. Hammering desert winds where you can feel the weight of the sun. Weather that doesn't care if it kills you. Weather that doesn't notice, this is a cruelty that attracts me.

To die alone in the cold on purpose. To be torn limb from limb by bears and dragged away to be eaten. To never have the bones or any remains whatsoever found. To me, this is beautiful. Better than the cheap filth drain of the contemporary city. Better than dying of television, cigarettes and dyed food. More meaningful than action movies and popular culture. There is no way to die with any honor in America. Soon there will be pay-per-view of the last moments of famous people. You will be able to watch the demise of your idols. It will be big as Court TV. They could have the day to day highlights and then the big blow out at the end when the person hits flat line. I'd pay to see Ronald Reagan die on television, where do I send the check?

She said I was primitive. Right then, I wanted to grab her by the hair and fuck her with my teeth embedded in her shoulder. I'm on a stage and I'm pulling my intestines out of a hole in my midsection while I tell jokes about my parents and how crazy they are. People are laughing at the jokes and don't seem to mind that I'm disemboweling myself in front of them. I tell them to hold on a second and step around the intestines and pull out a hand gun and shoot myself in the face twice and keep on going even though my mouth is partially destroyed by the bullets. People don't seem to mind or even notice. I finish the show and catch my breath backstage for about ten minutes. There is a knock at the door. It's the stage manager. He wants to know if it's alright to keep the kids inside who want to meet me. I tell him, "Sure, I'll be out in a few minutes." By this time, I have healed up pretty good and my intestines have grown back. You have to be tough in this business. You always have to be able to deliver whether you're sick or not into it, basically you're always on. It's always showtime. I go out and meet the people who have stayed after. They ask for autographs and to mutilate me. They always love to mutilate me. I tell them, sure. It's not as if they get to do it to their parents or teachers. As they stab me, they ask me to sign my name in the blood that's flowing from the wounds they are inflicting. I nod yes and do it. A young man asks if he can punch me in the face as hard as he can and I tell him, sure. He winds up and punches me in the face. I fall to the ground and they help me up. The young man thanks me and asks me to sign an arm of mine that he pulled off me in '85. I sign it and give it back. It was good to see that arm, it had been a long time. I try not to get sentimental about stuff like this because you can't get attached to any of it, drags you down you know? A young girl tells me that she has seen every show I've done in this town since 1982. I thank her. She asks if she can have a hug and then cut my head off because she has one of my heads from '91 and wants to make book ends. I tell her sure, at least the match will be pretty close. I don't think I look as good as I used to, all the traveling really takes it out of you. She hugs me and hacks my head off with the help of her boyfriend who tells me it's an honor. After my head is chopped off, I am lead away and taken to the hotel. I have to get some sleep. I have a show in another town the night after. I have to get my rest, it's the only thing that repairs me. Nothing like a good night's sleep.

Many have wasted themselves on you. They have squandered time, words and emotion. Destroyed their hearts with thoughts of you. The look in your eyes never changed. You never raised your voice but something inside was getting satisfied. You're proud that you never want them and they always want you. It is dark. You're walking alone. Your eyes are inexplicably drawn to your left. You see a dark human form walking quickly past. Your body grows cold and you wrap your coat tightly around yourself. You quicken your step to follow but you don't know why. As the shadowed form moves with increasing speed you are unable to walk normally. It is as if your feet are weighted. You call out. The form stops and looks back then continues on quickly disappearing into the night. There you stand, your feet riveted to the ground feeling rejection for the first time. It is me, the stranger. He who does not want. I cannot change or hide what I am even if I wanted to. Interrogation would not be necessary. I am branded in every possible way. It is the road I took that made me what I am. It is impossible, after a certain point, to go back to a previous way of life, a previous way of thinking. It is no longer an option. This makes things simple, if not calming. I tried to walk away from it a few times in the past. I was young and didn't understand the permanence of the marks the rites of my particular passage were leaving upon me. It is difficult to deal with contemporary attitudes with the ancient, often brutal perspective my path has provided. I must applaud myself for my use of unconscious restraint during the last few years when walking the streets of this decadent failure. Many is the time that someone has crossed the line and lost the privilege of respect. "Don't do anything unnecessary" flashes though my mind in situations like these and I let it pass. This maxim has always provided me with clarity in the quickly changing and often untenable urban setting. Over the din of traffic, my mind only hears the roar of the ocean. Where they see garbage, I see clusters of beautiful wild flowers. My mind is unpolluted by the decadence that reigns in the city. I am pointed at, called after and given many opportunities to be annoyed by these weak intrusions. What they don't know is that I only hear the howl of wind tearing across a high mountain top and that none of their words have meaning to me. They do not know what I stand for. They do not know my beliefs and what makes my spirit strong like iron and flexible like a young tree. "Never forget what you are" is something that I say to myself often lest I momentarily forget. It is important, you know, to never forget what you are. When you know what you are then no one can take anything from you. Of course, this is something that you will never be able to explain to anyone. There are of course, some obvious traits that pull you out from the numbing mediocrity of the masses: You never relent. Your unbelievable resolve is free from the malice of blind ambition. You can go without. You do not complain. You do not allow yourself to be compromised by the weakness of others. You only fight in self defense and when you do, it is unleashed with a hostile fury that is indescribable and only illustrates the respect you have for your own life. You can be alone for infinite periods of time. You are clear, grounded, intense and spontaneous. And you never forget what you are. Warrior.

You would have laughed about this. We were walking up a hill of the graveyard where your ashes are now buried. It was me and all of your relatives. I didn't know any of them. One of them, I guess one of your grandmothers or something (the one with the fake leg) lost her shoe on the hill and I was the one who was down on my knees getting it back on her plastic hoof. Nice enough lady. It was funny in the middle of all those gravestones. Your body was still in possession of the county. This was a few days before they burned you up and put you in the box. Oh yeah, your father goes on corny television shows now and implicates me in your death. I guess he's using you to put some life into his sagging career by working the sympathy angle. Pretty pathetic, but he always struck me that way. After awhile you make friends with the memories. They die down and lie at your feet and do not turn into snakes. It takes awhile to be able to laugh to yourself about something bad that happened. Humiliation is hard for me to swallow. I have had my share. Not as much or as bad as some people I have heard of but we all asked for it, so what the hell. Have you seen those television shows where the host gets people to come on to basically fight and argue with each other? They have topics such as: "Men who are married and have an affair with another woman and get her pregnant." They will find three sets of these three-way misery combos and bring them on so people can make fun of them and their family members can tear into them at will. The audience eats it up. It's like throwing a gazelle into piranha-infested water. The topics border on unreal. Women who think their sister is prettier than they are. They bring out two fat women in stretch pants to talk about how the other one makes the other one jealous and how she gets all the good men in town and all of this horseshit and you wonder where in the hell they get these people from. Then at the end of the show they give you a number to call if you fit the topic of the next upcoming show. These people definitely ask for it. It gives you an idea as to how many ugly and dumb people watch daytime television. The depths these people will sink to be on national television is incredible. I caught myself feeling sorry for the guy who was getting yelled at for making the fifteen year-old girl pregnant and then marrying her. The audience and the girl's parents were all saying mean things to him and he just sat there and kind of shrugged his shoulders. You realize these people are the talk of the town they live in when they return. Their lives become a play for the locals. Free beers and bowling for a few weeks and then things go back to normal. For these people, it was the biggest thing they ever accomplished. For the show, it was another stage full of idiots and there will be another load in tomorrow. Keep these idiots coming. The show will never have to worry about running low. To change topics rather quickly, my love for you will always be in the shadows. I like the fact that I see you fairly often and you have no idea as to how I feel about you. You don't know and you will never know. It's buried in the middle of this piece of writing and you'll never see it. Furthermore, even if you do see it, you'll never know that this pertains to you anyway. I will never tell you because the thought of having to make you hear me say it makes me feel horrible. I could never do that to you. I know the look on your face would be unbearable. It is because I feel so strongly for you that you will never know of this. I feel absolutely unlovable. I have for years. In fact, I am sure I am totally repellent. I had a dream where I told you how I felt about you threw your hands up to your face and screamed. It was then that I realized that twin jets of sulfuric acid had come squirting from my mouth and mutilated you. I try to move your hands from your face so I can help but my touch burns your skin and you beg me to get away. I try to kill myself but as hard as I try, I cannot make myself die. I throw myself off cliffs only to bounce back to the top where I can see you screaming and calling for help. When I try to come close, you crawl away and your screams make my ears bleed and I want to die for the terrible thing that I have done by telling you that I love you more than anything on the face of the earth. In the last part of the dream, I see the two of us from above and you're screaming and your flesh is smoking and I am running around with my hands to my ears with blood running through my fingers. It's a mess and no one gets better. I know it's only a dream but it told me all I needed to know. I'll never let you know how I feel. It will stay with me forever. And you know, it makes me love you even more. It makes you more beautiful to me. I like the version of you I have. I know that's selfish but that's all we get sometimes. We get the dream and sometimes we don't want to know the reality. You're in my thoughts always. From somewhere dark and remote, I protect and watch out for you.

You were a flower that smelled like gasoline. When you burst into flame, I could not let go. Your beauty and kindness cauterized you to me. You are with me always, mixed with my scar tissue, beneath my twisted skin. I threw myself off the chair I was sitting in. I compelled myself to the floor. I am below the windows. I can no longer take the view. Dull street and late morning haze. I am on my knees staring at the dirty carpet. My parents are blown out of existence and I know no one. I am trapped and sick under the cancerous skies. I can remember little of my past. All I can remember clearly are facts from a few hours ago and I repeat them over and over again just to hear myself think. I saw over six used condoms in the gutter on the way to the store. I saw one in a dog's mouth. The man walking the dog laughed and said, "Drop!" The palm trees are a paler shade of green in the winter. The sky was mute blue, idiotic and huge, torn by condominiums. The people in the market are getting sick from the food they buy week after week. Hungry as I was, I was unable to purchase any of the conspiracy product. I would feel safer living on a diet of aerosol sprays—anything that says it's harmful. I trust the bad news always. I came back to the room and broke down. I am beyond panic or sadness. No one's company could strip me of the mutiny that rips through me. The room takes on a different shape as I descend deeper into the sickness. It becomes small enough to crush my skull and then suddenly expands to leave me desolate and disconnected from everything. At this moment, I am a god because I defy all gods and all methods of order. I am of single no-mindedness. The people who live below, above and to my left and right have no idea of the howling cavern of darkness that lives on the other side of their walls. I am at the end of the vacuum. Seeing my life for the first time without the distractions fear brings. At this moment, I know the absolute truth and I am freezing cold but alright. Nothing that came before matters. It is obvious it taught me nothing. People just filled me full of screaming, expectation and ashes. I've fucked them, hit them, buried them, done everything to keep them around, everything possible to get them away from me and all it got me was here. So, people no more. I will train my thoughts to be assassins. They will kill memories of all who live in my brain. The thoughts will silently stalk and kill anyone they find. At the end of the day, I will have no memory of anyone. By the time the moon is in the sky, my mind will be empty of humanity. I will be pure. I will be silent. I will be powerful and will have no need to demonstrate. The only language I will need is whatever I am hearing inside me right now. Until my thoughts kill me, I remain lashed to myself.

I was standing on the sidewalk the other day watching people walk by. Two men walked by with their arms around each other's waists. One was wearing a large wig and intense makeup. He had high heels on and was having a bit of trouble walking. People came out of stores to look at the large black man dressed like a woman. The man saw me looking at his wig-wearing date, made his eyes into slits and hissed, "Jealous!" I knew right then and there that I would rather have love than money. I don't think we give ourselves enough credit. How we manage to live through our own wretchedness is beyond me. I think we should <u>all</u> get Nobel Peace prizes. Look at the slums and mansions we live in year after year. It's all perfectly obscene in its own way. Look at the things that we do to each other. Victims and the victimizers both in a unique and humiliating hell. Imagine Duke Ellington, one of the greatest talents in the history of the planet, hearing the roar of a standing room only audience absolutely ecstatic from what became known as the "Ellington Effect." All the while Duke is up there bowing and thanking the audience, he knows he can't stay in a hotel in town because of his skin color. He always told the audience he loved them madly. How could you love a bunch of people who would allow that while they clap and cheer in your face? *"Thank you, you fucking self-serving bigots! You're the greatest, most oppressive race the world has ever known! Excuse us now as we have to drive to the shittiest place in the city to stay the night! We'll see you again if we don't get lynched in the meantime!"* What if you were stupid enough to think that a black man was not fit to stay in the same hotel as a white man? Wouldn't the weight of that stupidity be hard to bear? Don't you think there is a moment when a Klansman has to pull off his hood, catch his breath and admit that his corny, white bread cracker bullshit is too much even for him to handle and that he is impossibly fucked up? So fucked up and ignorant that he should be awarded a prize for reaching such heights of self-inflicted retardation? Imagine the hell of working in a McDonald's. Imagine the hell of eating that crap. No one gets out of the punishment. Who was worse off: OJ, Nicole and Ron or the world that watched? We're all fucked! The Juice should get an award for Largest Catastrophe Perpetrated on a Nation by a Single Male. You have to admit, the trial was brilliant in its take-no-prisoners tactics. Take no prisoners. Get it?!! I kill me! I cut my head off with a steak knife!! A man you will never meet took up hours of your time and gave you nothing! He ruined families and turned up the heat on the already horrid race problem in this country. The "N-WORD"?! I am amazed that we survive each other and ourselves as long as we do. We are an elite species. Hats off to us and our stunning capacity to absorb and inflict cruelty!!

Some people will never know true love and I feel bad for them. They make the mistake of loving someone and telling them all about it. Whenever you bring in another person the whole thing is ruined. All you can do is screw it up from there on. I fall in love with the faces of women who pass me on the street. I imagine how it could be... until the next one passes and I'm in love again. No one gets hurt, no promises are broken. And what of the love? It's fleeting and intense like it should be. I don't need the physical act to make it real. That's like keeping the stuffed animal you won at the carnival. When you get it home, it has no place. I love the sound that comes out of John Coltrane's horn. The sound will never leave me. There will be no messy divorce papers. No screaming matches and acrimony, just endless love. Don't ever think I'm sleeping on the job. I'm out there, working for you every waking minute. Sometimes I have dreams where I am working for you too, so I guess that counts for something. I am here for your amusement and taunting. When you stare at me and make a scene,

I have no choice but to stand there and endure it when I would rather be hurting you, screaming at you to shut up. I just look at the floor and wait for you to get your fill and move on. I have changed all my habits because of you. I look down when I walk the streets. I go out at night because there's less of you out there. I have grown to like cold weather because I can wear clothes that obscure my identity. It's hard to take it when you touch me. I'll be in the store and all of a sudden one of you has your arm around my shoulder. You yell my name a few times in the small market and now everyone's staring. It's ok, you're drunk, or whatever you please. I can't have a problem with this. I just smile weakly and fight off the feeling of wanting to disappear or have it all just be a dream. I'm on a cheap display pedestal for your amusement so you can say later that I was short and an asshole but you always knew that anyway, so fuck it. There's always the one where you are surprised how "down to earth" I am when you meet me. I guess you expected me to be a jerk and you were amazed to see me buying a broom in a department store like a real person. I have been called on every crime and flaw, real or imagined. You all know me better than I do and know what's better for me as well. I do not feel proud of anything I have ever done in all my years as a performer. It's always been a tentative and edgy relationship I've had with you. After a few bottles in the head and too much humiliation, I just try to do my thing without getting too much on me. I don't think I have many real friends. Most of the people I know, I either pay a salary or a percentage to. The women I meet have read and heard everything I've ever done and that is the basis of our conversation or whatever else is in mind. I don't know if I have ever been with a woman who actually knew me. Don't think I ever feel any sense of accomplishment about many things I may have "done" in my life. I know it's all subject to your approval. I can work hard on something and in the end, its merit will be determined by strangers who get paid to fill paper with their lightweight opinions about something that took years to make. They're done with me in a few hundred words. All performers are pathetic to a certain degree. In order to get up there you have to have a little of that disgusting need for approval running through you. When you applaud my insecurities, it's the most ironic, horrible thing imaginable, and of course, I thank you. Without you, I would be nowhere. Without you, I would not exist. Because of you, there's me. I know that. I have known it the whole time. Like I said before, please don't think I'm slacking off. I'm always on the job. When I've just done a three and a half hour show and you wait outside because you need more, I'll look at your blank stare when I tell you I have about six hours before I have to go to the airport. I know you don't give a fuck. You want more. If I don't say thank you to every accolade and don't sign every piece of paper you put in my face, I'm a rockstar asshole who shits on his fans and not a tired human being who gave you everything he had. I know this is the way it is. Whenever I'm sitting in my room on my mattress wishing I could go outside but not feeling up to the constant barrage of voices, hands and stares, I think of you. When I look at the things I own, I think of you because you are the ones who provided me with them. I have no feeling of legitimate ownership of any of it. I figure I am one of those people who sunk low enough for you to put your foot on my neck and for that privilege, you gave me some money and I bought some things. I know it could all get taken away. Hard come, easy go. You don't hear me complain. I'm just stating the facts. You're buying it, I'm living it. I live on a diet of hope. The hope you'll like me. I have never felt like anything more than one of those dogs at a dog show with his nose and ass up in the air.

Help me to withstand your beauty as it stands out of reach. Give me the capacity to forget ever having felt your touch. Give me the courage to walk away before I destroy myself with self-inflicted torment while you are nowhere to be seen. I cannot find it in myself so I come to you. You, who led me away from my cave into the light. You, who told me it was alright to open myself to you and let my feelings come to the surface. You, who confused and left me out to dry. Please help me to forget you. I tend a lighthouse off the coast of Maine. I have lived and worked here alone for at least seven years. I don't keep track of time like I used to. After many nights listening to the furnace quietly hiss and looking out the window, time has no importance. I know sunrise-sunset, high-tide, low-tide. I know the bones inside my skin and the feeling of my teeth in my mouth. I sometimes wonder about what the people on a passing ship might think when they pass me in the middle of the night. I wonder if they think about the lighthouse keeper. I wonder if they laugh out loud and say it must be the worst job on earth. I wonder if any of them ever wave and wish me well. I do not go to the mainland for visits or supplies. Four boxes are brought out to me once a month by the runner at a supply store. I am always asked if I have any mail to send. I wonder why they still ask as I have never once sent or received a piece of mail. I have a phone that is to be used for emergencies. I have never had a ship in distress and have never used the phone once. I love the night and the roar of the sea. Some nights it's just me and the water's anger. I sit and silently marvel at its fury. I do not think of people I have known, for it's been so long I don't remember if I knew them. I have long since forgotten the names and faces. There were women but they never made me remember them or want to go back to them. I always felt they were talking to someone else when they were talking to me. I never asked them about that; I never saw the point. I have never been married. I have never been in love with anything human. I love the salt filled air and nights spent looking at the moon. Even when I was working in a kitchen or cleaning offices, my thoughts were always of the sea and a lighthouse on a rocky, inhuman coastline. These thoughts gave me strength to withstand the daily humiliation and degradation that is a big part of dealing with the human race. I figured the longer I was amongst them, the more I would become like them. I was disgusted at their weakness and terrified of their thoughtless violence. The brainless throng walking the streets, yelling and insulting each other. One day I saw a man get hit by a car and another man take his wallet while a pool of blood formed around his head. He told the unmoving onlookers he was looking for his identification cards to help him when the ambulance came. A few people nodded. He walked to the edge of the crowd unnoticed and slipped away. I don't know what became of the man. I came up here and relieved a young couple of this job. They wanted to try it out for a year to test their relationship. I think that's what they said. I just smiled and nodded and learned the job. I was relieved to see them leave. I slept in the back room and left the windows open to rid the small house of their smell. I packed all the books and magazines away in the back room and the place was perfect. Through no work on my part, all my memories started to fade into a blur that held absolutely no interest to me. People live in the past all their lives. They replay instances over and over and rarely live life without the insulation of the past to keep them secure. Instead of walking they take cautious, trembling steps, always looking over their shoulder to make sure the past is close by. They drag people from their past with them so they can have a sympathetic reminder of a time before they were afraid. I wanted something else. I wanted to see how real life plays out and what thoughts I would have if I wasn't occupied with the voices and opinions of others. What are people? Breathing reflections of what they love, hate and fear.

That is not enough for me. Thoughts of them make me feel tired and weighted down. I live for the setting sun and the night with the sea and the bell and the wind. I am the keeper of the light. I keep you safe from a shoreline that would tear your craft to bits and dash your brains all over the rocks for the crabs and gulls to eat.

I'm coming back as the center of an archway that will someday, inexplicably come loose and fall, only killing the innocent. She appeared in different forms over the years. All deadly. All beautiful. Coming closer. In dreams and in passing. And there I was. Desperate for a woman to just breathe on me. Desperate like thousands of nights alone will make you. You will see visions. You will believe she holds the power to heal. You will believe anything she tells you. And you will want her more than life itself because she is the only thing that makes life possible. She reached out to touch me. My flesh felt like an ancient wound being healed. Imagine how little I suspected her intention. Imagine how pathetic my smile must have been. How powerful my embrace, my desperation apparent. Imagine the depth and peace of my sleep. When I awoke, my blood had been drained and placed in bottles that formed a line next to the body. She stood in front of me, silently laughing. I asked her if I was alive. She said no, just in love and proceeded to smash my face with a hammer. *Snakes and my freezing hands. Staying out late. Walking miles through concrete worlds. Trying to freeze it to death. Trying to get better. Trying to understand how you can be ripped to pieces over and over and still come up breathing, ready to stand in line with all the others. Looking at the faces of the humans passing by and wondering if they have had their blood drained and their faces smashed in with hammers. Is humiliation genetic? Was it something I was taught while I was a child?* She appears again. I point my finger and tell the truth. Humans rush at me, calling me names and threatening me. I am left with hammer holes in my brain and the scorn and hatred of strangers.

I have to tell you this quickly because I do not know how much longer I will last. I don't know what will take me first. Thirst or unconsciousness. It doesn't matter with blood loss and head wounds, one or the other will get you. You are a perfect audience. From my left eye, I can see you are strapped to a chair as I am. I do not know what happened to my right eye. I cannot raise my hands to feel. I don't know if I lost it or if the lids are stuck together with blood. Can you hear me? You are nodding. Yes, you can hear me. Before I begin, I must ask you how you got here. Well, why don't you speak? Have they ripped out your tongue? Oh. I'm so sorry. The pain must have been incredible. I wonder if you had a tongue to speak with if you would tell me to be silent. So many times people speak to others who do not want to hear. So much for good intention. I must hope you do not wish for my silence. Sometimes all we want is someone to hear us. Someone to be there to nod and raise their eyebrows. Not necessarily to understand, accept or sympathize but merely to bear witness. Pathetic I know but life is such a lonely road. My friend, my friend, are you alright? Are you trying to scream? Don't struggle against the restraints, your bleeding will only get worse. So where shall I begin? It has always bothered me that Kafka's woman burned a portion of his work after his death as was his wish. Imagine! So much we will never know... It's a dirty trick they played on me. It must have been some kind of military experiment. They're always using life as an experiment, as a chess piece. Expendable. It must have been a long time ago. So long ago I cannot remember being deposited here on this planet. Maybe my brain was operated on to eliminate memories of the past. Yes, it was a horrible thing to do to me, to leave me here with no idea of how to get back to where I came from and no memory of where it is. Was I put here to explore and get data? Was I supposed to round up samples to take back to them? I don't know. I have no idea whatsoever what I am doing here and what will happen to me. For as long as I can remember, I have just gone along with it and tried not to raise the suspicion of the inhabitants. It's been easy enough, they're so easily convinced of anything. I can use their words, their language is the only one I know. This is infuriating because I know the one I was born with had to be much more complex and satisfying. I can speak all day long but never say anything. I have absolutely no recollection of what my own ideas were like. I think to myself and at the same time, I know these thoughts can't be the ones I really want to think. That there must be something better to have on my mind than what fills it and refuses to stop occupying all the room. I eat their food. I pay with their currency. I earn money doing their tasks. I do not love or hate them. I only fear them and hope someday I will meet one of my own kind.

Ten thousand ton suffocating night, I'm so glad you're here to pound all the sense out of my head. I'm so relieved the pain is finally over. It has been hard to carry it all day after day. Now I know there is life after she leaves. Now when I hear men singing the blues on the radio, I think they're suckers when I used to feel the same way. All those songs about waiting for her to come back. I lived the lyrics. I waited for her to come back. I stuffed myself like an animal in a trophy shop and waited in the window. Where she went and where she is are facts I don't know and don't care if I ever know. If she called me right now I would be polite and tell her I understand and she doesn't have to explain a thing. I know the truth. You do what you have to do. The way you are is the way you are and I am not here to judge you and your actions. Thank you, putrid choking urine stench Night. Thank you, men

falling out of doorways looking for change. Darkness. I owe you big time garbage strewn alleys of failure and damnation painted by moonlight scene. Because of walking through you, I see clearly. I got my sight back from your destitute hunchbacked monster sleeping on a grate perspective. I see what. I see how. I see why. I know the truth. I no longer need. Take the bandages off my skin and let me out of the iron lung. Tell the burn ward I won't be coming back for treatment. Tell the doctor in intensive care I won't be getting that amputation. I am healed. I am screaming. I am smiling like Buddha out of malice and clarity. Now that I am at the end of my life, I have found it necessary to take stock of all the things I learned and all the experiences I had. I want to know what kind of man I am, was and could have been. The one thing that is clear in my mind, even in the state I am in, which must be far less than up to speed, is that one will always dwell upon what he could have been rather than what he is. The things he never became take on legendary, mythical proportions, a specter that stands over him, eclipsing the actual events of his life. Realizing my ultimate conclusion will be mainly determined by how others have judged me, I go on, knowing the result will be somewhat tainted with their opinion no matter how objective I try to be.

I see now the anger I had towards my parents at the way they raised me played a large part in how I treated others and especially the women I encountered. Never once did I ever confront my mother or father about the pain and misery they probably unknowingly heaped upon me when I was young. I always saw it as weak to complain about anything that was bothering me. I always thought it better to hold it inside and let it resolve itself.

The last time I saw or spoke to either one of my parents was well over ten years before they died. Growing up, they never told me much about themselves and in later years the estrangement only widened the gap between us. I barely remember their voices.

Sometimes flashes of memories come back briefly, but almost as fast as they come, they vanish.

And how did this affect the relationships I had with women? I never trusted them. I could never commit to just one. In my mind I knew a woman would abandon me and inflict cruelty as my mother had. I found it impossible to stay with one woman. I could never take their word seriously as I could never take anything my mother said for truth. All I remember was the divorces, the yelling matches between them as they ravaged each other. The idea of marriage and children filled me with claustrophobic fear. When I saw couples with their children, I always figured they were all miserable and hiding it well for appearance's sake as my parents and I had done. So I never got married and was never monogamous.

Only a few times out of the many women I was with, did I ever feel anything besides momentary lust, low level contempt and sometimes, pity. Never shame, though. No matter how I might have hurt a woman's feelings, I know somewhere sometime, she had done the same or worse to someone else. That's one thing I think about when I look at people walking on the street. Almost all of them have caused someone else great pain with their acts of betrayal, rejection or some other form of brutality. Even a greater percent, perhaps all, have suffered at the hands of another human at some point. I wonder how many women I have met have been raped. Imagine carrying that around like a grenade lodged in your throat.

I never raped a woman. I never hit one either. One woman told me if I really loved her, I would hit her. She actually wanted me to do it. I remember telling this to another man and he asked me if I did and when I told him no, he was amazed.

I like the way the sunlight comes into the window in my room. I don't get out much anymore. I like to sit and watch people pass by across the street. It's a good street. If it has changed any in the last however many years I have been here, I am not aware of it. I am not aware of many things anymore but that's fine with me. It took me almost to the end of my life to realize ninety-nine percent of the things I learned and was concerned with were a waste of time. If I knew then what I know now, I would have been a better person. Not so out for myself all the time. Ambition, what a rotten-to-the-core concept that is.

I can still remember the streets of my youth. I have not been back there in over thirty years. I guess I won't be getting back there. That's the kind of thought I have been finding profound. Never going back there again. I never thought like that before. Why won't I be going back there? Because I will die before I get the chance? Because I don't want to? How many things have I done for the last time? I remember all the last times I spoke to people before they died. I have an uncanny memory for that and I don't know why. It's not as if I knew it was going to be the last time I spoke to them.

And why am I thinking of these things now? Were they always in my head and just waiting until the right time? It is calming to know after I am gone, someone else will be occupying this room. It's not as if they are going to level the building in my honor.

A few nights ago, I woke up in the middle of a deep sleep with the panicked need to contact someone. I felt alone. There was a tightness around my throat. I spent at least an hour trying to remember someone I knew who wasn't the man at the store or my accountant. I could think of no one. Sometimes I see people I have spoken to or met briefly in magazines, usually after they have passed away. Every once in awhile, when someone I knew dies, my accountant usually sends me a letter on his very professional letterhead regretting to tell me that so and so has passed away. Why is it the accountant who sends me these things? Is he the one I told I never read newspapers or watch television? Strange term that, passed away. If you ever saw the people I used to associate with, you would never think of them passing away. Either they get killed or they die, they don't pass away. The accountant, he'll pass away.

As for myself, I don't know how I will go. When I was younger, I of course, had my sights on a legendary career topping exit. Something fiery, like taking out numerous law officials as I went out in a blaze of glory. For many years my concept was to go out to the arctic and walk until I froze to death and live the last few minutes of my life in full knowledge I was dying alone with no one to witness. I wondered what thoughts I would think. It all sounded so romantic as it bounced off the walls of my skull.

It's something the way our access to history has changed over the years. I can see videos of myself from fifty years ago. I have a closet full of videos, records, news clippings. I never look at them but a few times some people have come by to look and borrow things for some documentary they did about my life. I have that in the closet as well. Never seen it. Never will. It was bad enough to be that guy. I don't want to see what they think I was. They'll never know how much of it was bullshit. That the crowds were smaller and the glory was elusive and only noticed when it had gone.

When people recognize me on the street, it's funny. An old man telling another old man how he used to go wild to the music. Two old men nodding and shifting on their tired feet. It's times like that when I am sure I made many mistakes with my life. I let too much matter. How much time we waste thinking about what others think of us. All the time I wasted talking to the press. What a vain bunch we all were. We were all in a play. Amazed at the power we thought we held. I wonder what I would have done with all the time had I spent it more wisely. It doesn't matter now.

My parents have been dead so long I have forgotten what it was like to know they were alive. I never knew them, they never knew me. I didn't go to the funerals. Didn't show up for the reading of the wills. Never responded to calls from the relatives. Never felt a thing outside of some curiosity about these people who raised me. They matter as much as what day it is today. It's all the same, just facts, names, morals and rituals. The more of them you miss, forget and ignore the better.

All about Maya: Maya was the most intense woman I ever met in my life. She scared me and she knew it. I met her when she was hanging out with a guy I was in a band with. She went out with him a couple of years before. Now they had one of those loose relationships. She would come by where we used to live and practice. She and my buddy would go somewhere to fool around. She used to drag him away by his belt. I used to hate the helpless look he would get when she did that.

She turned tricks when she needed money for drugs which was most of the time. Once, she came by the place and asked us if we were hungry. We were always hungry in those days. She smiled and said she would be back soon. In a few hours she returned with a bag of food from a delicatessen. I asked her where she got it from and she laughed at me like the witch she was and yelled, "Turning tricks you fuckhead!"

She then made a grab for my dick. I always teased her about not wanting to get leprosy from her. This just made her fuck with me more.

"Come on you little faggot. I should get one of my stud friends to come over and fuck you good. I know that's what you want. Come here you little chicken."

She knew this shit would make me leave the room. She always won.

I saw her one day walking crookedly west up Santa Monica Blvd., thumbing down eastbound traffic. She was wearing high heels, fishnet stockings held up with garter belts hooked to black panties. She had on a tank top that had a red swastika on the front. Her makeup was running and she looked like hell. A car picked her up across the street from Astro Burger. Off they went. I didn't bother to tell my friend about it. He never talked about the crazy shit she got up to and no one ever brought it up when he was around. It's not like he didn't know she fucked and sucked in the alleys and parking lots of Hollywood.

A few days later, we got a call from a clinic near the airport. Maya was there with a broken jaw. A john had punched her in the face in lieu of payment. Our number was the only one she knew. I remember the look on my friend's face. Tired and resolved. He silently took the keys to the van and went to get her. He didn't bring her back and none of us asked where he put her.

I didn't see or hear about her for a couple of years after that. The next I heard about her was another call from a clinic. Someone had broken her jaw again and as an added bonus, she was pregnant and had hepatitis. My friend went off and dealt with it.

A few months later she wound up on our doorstep. A few hours into her appearance at our hovel, she had dragged two old men back from a corner bar and serviced them in our bathroom. None of us had the guts to ask her not to bring clients back to our place. Finally, one of us asked her and she was amazingly cool about it. With Maya, any coolness was just the calm before a storm. That night she took a can of contact cement and got high with it in the bathroom and passed out. We broke in and got the glue-drenched t-shirt off her face and took her outside for some fresh air. She was mad at us for saving her. She said she wanted to die and we were motherfuckers for stopping her. The next night she found the glue can and went off to a nearby field with it. One of the guys was walking to the store and thought he saw her in the field and ran over to her. She was passed out with a small towel dipped in glue next to her face. Again, we revived her. She took off the next day after cussing us all out and taking a few swings at me.

The next time I saw her was a year later in Hollywood. She was living with a fellow junkie and prostitute. A slim guy named Benny. He had bleached blonde hair and worked the stretch of Santa Monica Blvd. called "Boystown." The last time I saw her, I teased her that she and Benny could share clothes. The last time I heard about him, he had gone out on a drug scoring mission and got snuffed. I never heard from or about Maya again. That was ten years ago.

Maya once told me about a girl who she helped to commit suicide. She was a friend of Maya's. I think the girl bought drugs from her. Most of the people she knew were either prostitutes or drug addicts doing small crime to get the money to score. Anyway, this young girl wanted to check out so Maya sold her some downers and took her to Errol Flynn's old mansion, which was at this point a pile of rubble and an empty pool at the top of a hill in Hollywood. The place was frequented by a wild crowd that liked to party there. I went up there a few times but it didn't do anything for me. A bunch of guys getting high and scary girls getting fucked in the bushes. During the day this place was deserted. Maya took the girl up there one afternoon and fed her the pills and made her wash it down with a lot of milk. Maya said it helped you die better. I don't know what that means but that's what she said. The girl choked on her vomit and died. Maya watched. She tossed off this story like she was talking about her shoes. Like it was nothing.

To withstand your weakness and tyranny I had to become a virus. When you introduce a new vaccine, I mutate and you are back to square one. You are infuriated and awed by my simple act of survival at what you think are impossible odds. You don't see your down side. You're too busy taking it all in. All those

different channels, the variety of rape and abuse you are addicted to. You couldn't concentrate on one thing if your life depended on it. You could be getting eaten by a shark and you would still check your beeper to see who was calling you. When it comes to containing me, your words don't work. Your culture is sterile against me. Your crumpled up designer expression is nothing but a fashion statement. Your hurdles are but curbs in my path. I work to keep the shadows from my room. I don't live in the present or think of the future. Neither have anything to do with me. Where it's going is not where I'm going and where it is, I am not. I only have my past. I subsist on slowly decaying screams and fading horror. Rope burns of humiliation, failure and shame. If there were victories in my life I don't remember them and I think I would have. So many nights I have spent walking the streets thinking of one great thing I can do before I die. I want to do something I can be proud of. Something heroic maybe. It was yesterday when it hit me. The best thing I can do is be partially responsible for ending something horrible. It was then I knew I would never have children. It's not an idea I ever gave much thought to either way. I don't think any woman has ever looked at me and thought I was the one she would want to breed with. It is the ultimate way to end the race of my parents. I was the only child. I can single handedly bring their kind to an end. It's the way to kill them without taking the rap. I am already doing a life sentence but at least it's outside of a building full of mad men and victims of society. It's the only way to go out strong. By not having a family, my parents will never see their kind have another chance to see the light of day. I end them. I win without fighting. I kill by denying life. I exist in a living, breathing state of victory. I think of the two of them looking at me and me looking back smiling, shaking my head slowly. And in that instant, I know, they know. We know what we are.

The crowd gathered around the body and took everything they could. Clothes, watch, wallet, gold fillings. They left happy. The vultures came and consumed the flesh until they were full and flew away screeching with delight. The insects came and picked the bones clean. The sun bleached the bones white. The skeleton got up laughing and walked away. The best way I have found to disguise myself is to seemingly reveal everything about myself to them. When they think there is no more to get from me, they leave me alone and stop thinking about me. That's when I become free to do what I want. I am no longer curious to them and I bore them because they think they have all I have to offer. A long time ago I realized people only care about themselves and only feel safe around those they feel somehow superior to. People are afraid of cops but they feel superior to them because they think somehow cops work for them. Some make the mistake of thinking I am brave to tell them so much, when in reality, I don't tell them much about myself at all. I just play them back at themselves. It's what they want to hear because it makes them feel good. Only an idiot would trust someone else with information about themselves they would mind reading in the papers. The only time you are really free is when they think they have you captured and tagged. You get so close to them you disappear. Slip in, slip under, slip out. I never felt like I could ever be part of their world. I knew though, I would have to live in it. That's why I made sure they would never have me by making them think they already did. Defeat according to their rules may very well be a victory according to yours.

Get to the ritual. I don't care how many times it's been done. It's different when you're doing it. Get the paint on your face. Get the rage in your blood. Do the dance. Find the others. See their bodies move. There's power in movement. There's freedom in dance. It still works. The ancient ways are the best. There's a photo of two people. He's in a tuxedo. She's in a prom dress. The photo was taken in her parents' living room. He is putting a corsage on her left arm. She is smiling and looking directly into the camera. He is looking slightly off to one side. His eyes are slightly glazed over. He looks like he might have been drinking. *I remember going to my senior prom. There was no excitement about it. I went with a knee-jerk nothing-to-do that night variety of resolved boredom. It meant a bit more to my date. I rented the stupidest tuxedo I could find. A real old one with long tails. I looked like Groucho Marx. I forget what she wore. I picked her up at her mother's house. I felt like a stuffed animal. Every step I took felt like I was following painted footsteps on the floor.* He is wearing a scarf. It is hanging on either side of his neck. Her wrap is sitting on the left arm of a rocking chair. *When we got there we saw that not many people from my class had showed up. I immediately ditched my date and jumped up onstage and tried to sing "Soul Man" with the band. One of the horn players shoved me off the side while he was playing. I only danced to two songs. I danced with the headmaster's wife, knowing it would make him mad. And with my date, I danced to "Stairway to Heaven," the last song of the night. By that time, the only people in the place were a few bored teachers, some jocks, some geeks and the band. It was a depressing waste of time. I got my date back to her house as quickly as I could and jammed back to my neighborhood to try find my friends and make the most of the tragic waste of a Saturday night spent with losers, teachers and a date who worshipped Fleetwood Mac.* The boy and the girl are from Michigan. On the back of the picture there's a sentence written in black ink: "Shot himself in the head."

Obliterate me. Touch me into oblivion. Extinctionize me. Smother me when I fall asleep next to you. But please, make my last few moments memorable. Tell me something good before you put the

plastic bag over my head. If I am to love only once and only for a little while, if I am your little insect man, please set a good trap. Experience has hemmed me in. I have become addicted to the image of myself. I have become addicted to experiencing pure nothingness. With every breath, I withdraw further into my own experience until the world around me merely becomes an extension of me. The building exists so I can walk into it. The fact that others walk in as well is just because they are necessary to keep my experience alive and constantly moving, torturing me. I have tried to escape myself and have failed every time. Every voice, movement and face makes me more aware, more in need of distance from the experience of processing the information.

In an urban setting, noise is ever-present. I am constantly being victimized by sheer volume. The sight of the ugly buildings forcing themselves rudely and obscenely into the sky is terrifying. At intersections I stare at the ground for fear of being paralyzed by the intensity of the experience of the information.

I live for the relief of sleep where I dream of a soundless, sightless, informationless coma state. That would be the ultimate state of being for me. To have no thoughts, no thoughts of thoughts. No memory, no knowledge of anything.

The sound of human voices tells me to go into larval state with no intention of hatching. Curl up and be silent in the grey room. Dream of cement. Cement being poured into the room. I am at the bottom lying on a mattress. I am the hole in the drain. I am the darkness in the center of the dark room. I am that into which darkness pours itself in and loses itself. Solipsist, motherfucker. Yeah, the world is an extension of me. You're living in my vision.

In my dream, my friend has been murdered and I have to dispose of his body five different ways. First, I burn him. I go back into the

room expecting it to be over with but he's still there. He asks me what's going on, why I burned him. I tell him he's dead and he has to be burned because his father wants it that way and then I have to come up with four other ways to dispose of him. He asks me why I hurt him and I keep trying to tell him I don't want to hurt him but we have to do this. I never get to the second way. In another dream, I walk around the streets looking for him because I don't think he's dead but just moved to another place in the city. I think if I keep looking, a door in the darkness will open and I will walk through it and he'll be there and we'll laugh at everything like we used to. I have several hundred acres of property in the desert. In the middle of the land is a house in which I live. Instead of having bare wasteland to look at, I have brought in several tons of wreckage. Twisted car bodies litter the barren expanse. Every piece of airline wreckage I can buy or otherwise appropriate is strewn all over. When I look out the window, all I can see is the marriage of human ingenuity and error that caused death. Man destroying life in things made by other men is as close as we get to being gods, I think. Mechanized destruction of soft human tissue is beautiful. In the evenings when the sun is setting, I walk through the smashed statues of metal. I admire the engineering as it sits raped and rusting. Dried blood from the victims is visible, thanks to the sealant I covered the stains with. I never want to doubt man's frailty. I feel it is important to be humble. The dried blood is there to remind me of man's blind faith and arrogance. At night, I sit on the front porch and watch the moon shine down on the metal. Coyotes wander through the maze of mistakes, miscalculations and hulls that briefly housed screams and polarized moments of indescribable human terror. These monuments of death and destruction teach me more about man and life than anything I have ever known. Somehow I feel part of all this and at the same time, completely removed as I stare out at these silent shapes that reflect the moon like hundreds of pale eyes.

Other books from 2.13.61:

HENRY ROLLINS / The First Five
HENRY ROLLINS / Black Coffee Blues
HENRY ROLLINS / See A Grown Man Cry — Now Watch Him Die
HENRY ROLLINS / Get In The Van
HENRY ROLLINS / Eye Scream
HENRY ROLLINS / Do I Come Here Often?
JOE COLE / Planet Joe
DON BAJEMA / Reach
DON BAJEMA / Boy In The Air
BILL SHIELDS / Human Shrapnel
BILL SHIELDS / The Southeast Asian Book Of The Dead
BILL SHIELDS / Lifetaker
BILL SHIELDS / Rosey the Baby Killer
EXENE CERVENKA / Virtual Unreality
EXENE CERVENKA & KEN JARECKE / Just Another War
IAN SHOALES / Not Wet Yet
IGGY POP / I Need More
ELLYN MAYBE / The Cowardice of Amnesia
ART FEIN / L. A. Rock nad Roll History Tour
TRICIA WARDEN / Brainlift
TRICIA WARDEN / Attack God Inside
MICHAEL GIRA / The Consumer
ROB OVERTON / Letters To Rollins
NICK CAVE / King Ink
NICK CAVE / King Ink II
NICK CAVE & THE BAD SEEDS / Fish In A Barrel
ALAN VEGA / Cripple Nation
ROSS HALFIN / Fragile: Human Organs
ROSS HALFIN / Metallica: The Photographs of Ross Halfin
STEPHANIE CHERNIKOWSKI / Dream Baby Dream
THE PHOTOGRAPHER'S LED ZEPPELIN
ROKY ERICKSON / Openers II
JOE CARDUCCI / Rock & the Pop Narcotic
NICK ZEDD / Totem Of The Depraved
HENRY MILLER / Dear Dear Brenda